+2

Praise for Sales Success in Tough 1

"A truly excellent book which will not on for Salespeople, but I believe almost any and greater achievement."

RICHARD DENNY,
DAILY MAIL'S 'GURU OF MOTIVATION',
NATIONAL CONVENTION SPEAKER AND BEST-SELLING AUTHOR.

"Laurie's style is very much a gentle, guiding but informed hand on the shoulder, showing us the way. This is very important, because those who adopt a hard, aggressive approach to Sales Training have completely mis-read the current marketplace and economic situation. After reading the book, I felt I had under-gone a full service and MOT, essential for busy sales professionals!"

TOM PEARSON,
SALES DIRECTOR, JUPITER UNIT TRUST MANAGERS LTD.

"This book is about helping people in sales today – not some past era where slick sales lines and 'power phrases' were all one needed to succeed. It's packed with usable hints and tips, drawn from Laurie's own experiences in financial services, on how to succeed and thrive in today's challenging market-place. If you're looking for inspiration from someone, who like many of us, has sometimes doubted his own self-worth but has then risen to become one of the best, this is essential reading."

JOHN JOHNSON,
EXECUTIVE DIRECTOR, LIGHTHOUSE GROUP PLC
& SALES DIRECTOR, TEMPLE FINANCIAL PLANNING LTD.

"Laurie's advice is both passionate and pragmatic and often made me smile. His emphasis on Customer Service, especially in tough times, is spot on."

IAN GILMOUR,
GENERAL MANAGER, MGM ASSURANCE.

"Laurie's enthusiasm is infectious. This excellent book provides practical, humorous and ethical advice based on a lifestyle rooted in right values and vision. It is a must, a shot in the arm for even the most tired and frustrated salesman."

JOHN NOBLE,
CHAIRMAN LINKS INTERNATIONAL,
INTERNATIONAL CONFERENCE SPEAKER, AUTHOR & BUSINESSMAN.

"A MUST for Indian professionals seeking to do business with the West. The book gives clear and profound insights into the western mind-set. Any Indian reading this book will have a distinct competitive edge over his rivals!"

JOBEN ROY MYRBOH,
MANAGING DIRECTOR, MEGHALAYA STATE INDUSTRIAL CORPORATION, INDIA.

> Special discounts on bulk copies of this book are available. For details, please contact the Publishers.

Dream Depot Ltd.
P.O. Box No. 3218
Littlehampton, West Sussex, BN16 1WH
Tel: +44 (0)1903 859993
Fax: +44 (0)1903 859066
E-mail: office@dreamdepot.co.uk

First Published in Great Britain, October 2003
by Dream Depot Ltd.

ISBN: 0-9545979-0-7

Cover, text and cartoons designed and produced
by HEADWEST DESIGN Tel: 01903 733611.
Cover image supplied by the Corbis Corporation.
Covers printed by Oxted Colour Printers Ltd Tel: 01883 712351.
Text printed by Butler & Tanner Ltd Tel: 01373 451500.

A CIP Catalogue record for this books is available
from the British Library.

DREAM
DEPOT

SALES SUCCESS IN TOUGH TIMES

How to thrive, not just survive

LAURIE MELLOR

DREAM
DEPOT

The following Organisations and individuals were kind enough to give permission for the reproduction of previously published material:

Extracts from '*THE MONEY OR YOUR LIFE*' by John Clark, published by Century. Used by permission of The Random House Group Ltd.

Extracts from '*MOTIVATE TO WIN*' by Richard Denny, published in 1993 by Kogan Press Ltd.

Extracts from '*WORKING WITH EMOTIONAL INTELLIGENCE*' by Daniel Goleman © 1998 published by Bloomsbury.

Extracts from '*THE R FACTOR*' by Michael Schluter & David Lee published in 1993 by Hodder & Stoughton.

Every effort has been made to ensure that proper credit has been given for all sources used in this book. However, the Publisher has tried without success to contact the following copyright owners and would be pleased to hear from him/her so that the matter may be finalised:

'*SELLING WITH NLP*' by Kerry L Johnson published by Nicholas Brealey Publishing Ltd.

'*THE 7 HABITS OF HIGHLY SUCCESSFUL PEOPLE*' by Stephen R Covey, published by Simon & Schuster UK Ltd.

'*K.I.S.S. GUIDE TO SELLING*' by Ken Lloyd Ph.D, published by Dorling Kindersley Publishing.

About the Author

Laurie Mellor was born in 1948 and educated in London, at Ealing College and Kingston University, graduating with an honours degree in Social Science.

He has spent 20 years in sales, both in management and selling roles and is still active at the sharp end, so he is no armchair theorist. An Executive Consultant with Temple Financial Planning (part of the Lighthouse Group plc) for over 10 years, he is one of only three Salesmen in the Company's 35 year history to have achieved over £1 million gross commission.

Recently Salesman of the Year and invariably one of the top 5 consultants in the Company, he is a regular speaker at National and International Conventions; also an accomplished writer and columnist on sales and motivational topics.

Laurie has travelled extensively, especially in India and Africa and this enables him to bring a broader perspective to the subject; he is passionate about Customer Service and the need to build *real* relationships with clients.

Married with two children, he lives on the Sussex coast and lists reading, writing, music and cricket amongst his interests. He does not have a cat or a dog and his eldest son Sam describes him as *'a good bloke'*.

C O N T E N T S

Acknowledgments

I would like to mention the following who have in some way contributed to the writing of this book.

My current wife Brenda for her encouragement and support. Jack and Jay for a great start in life.

David Avery, my first boss in Financial Services, who believed in me and was diplomatic about my bright green suits.

Chris Staight, Marc Knight, Richard Hubbard, Richard and Belle Tongper, Neil Kealey, Trevor Magee, Tim and Donna Garman, David Thatcher, Bob Barnett.

Mike and Pat Jones for telling me to get on with it and then making it possible!

Richard Temple for his encouragement.

Terry Fisher – no longer with us – for being a father figure and the first to encourage me as a writer.

Derek Gardiner for believing in me and whose wise words came true.

John Noble for his wisdom and spiritual input.

Richard Denny for demonstrating that sales training could have integrity.

All my colleagues at Temple Financial Planning.

Paulo Coelho for showing me to follow my dreams.

Mike Seymour – that chance meeting in Ealing Broadway, London that changed my life.

God, who straightens our lives out and all my friends at Arun Community Church.

Foreword

Rather than attempt a slick, tailored, quote I felt it would be far more helpful to give the reader my thoughts, straight from the heart.

Sales Professionals always know that they should spend more time stepping back and re-examining their game plans, but to be honest, we NEVER do it enough. Look at the cover of the book. Do we stand in front of the mirror fully clothed and have a really good look at ourselves? I felt that when we do stand in front of that mirror, Laurie is asking us to be naked, such is the honest approach that he takes.

Laurie explores every nook and cranny of the sales arena and after reading the book, I felt I had under-gone a full service and MOT, essential for busy sales professionals. There were many moments when I felt I was reading about myself, but he asks us to face up to parts of our weird lives in sales that many of us would prefer to bury.

Laurie's style is very much a gentle, guiding but informed hand on the shoulder, showing us the way. This is very important, because those who adopt a hard, aggressive approach to Sales Training have completely mis-read the current marketplace and economic situation.

I thoroughly enjoyed the book and would strongly recommend it to you. It is fresh, easy to read with a distinct lack of psycho-babble. Laurie's gentle but informed approach is exactly what is needed for these tough times.

TOM PEARSON,
SALES DIRECTOR, JUPITER UNIT TRUST MANAGERS LTD, LONDON.

For Brenda,
Sam & Jamie

*"Hey Mr Dream Seller,
where have you been. . . .?"*

SALES SUCCESS IN TOUGH TIMES

How to thrive, not just survive

LAURIE MELLOR

MENU FOR SUCCESS

So how do we turn things around? How can we achieve Sales Success in Tough Times?

Here is the Menu. I hope you enjoy the meal!

Appetizers

In this section, you will hopefully find something to whet your appetite and to remind you why this book is important to you as a sales professional.

Starters

We will concentrate on the **inside** of the Salesman, not the external factors. You will find a total absence of 'sales techniques', but a wealth of advice on developing relationships with customers.

Before you can understand others, you have to understand yourself. No psychiatrist's couch, but practical insights in getting to know yourself better. Your greater skill in 'reading' your customers will have a *dynamic* impact on sales.

I will challenge you to be honest with yourself, looking at your weaknesses and helping turn them into strengths. Marketable strengths that will earn you more money.

Main Course

Great Salesmen lead with their hearts, and the Chapters on Emotional Intelligence will sharpen your intuition so that selling becomes much easier. We will cover areas such as self-management, motivation and social skills which will give you powerful new selling tools for your Recession-Buster Sales Toolkit.

I will help you unlock the secrets of the 'Jewel in the Crown' of Emotional Intelligence: **Empathy.** No pseudo-scientific 'techniques' or pyscho-babble, but powerful, pragmatic wisdom that will take your relationships with customers onto a deeper level, where they trust you and buy more from you.

I will show you how to motivate yourself, especially in tough times. How to strengthen your drive to achieve. How to set and achieve realistic goals.

I will stress why it is so important not to neglect existing customers: they are the 'diamonds under your feet' which you can turn into more sales.

Dessert

I will help you become a true professional on the telephone. If you are desperate to turn things round quickly, feel free to have this as your starter instead of your dessert.

I will help you dynamically improve your Customer Service Skills for the future.

No service charge is added to the bill:
the cover price of the book is sufficient.

Chapter One

APPETIZERS

WHY DID YOU
BUY THIS BOOK?

I would guess that the title struck a chord with you: you and I recognise that these are tough times. Tougher, perhaps, than you've ever known.

I'm glad you bought the book, because I think I have some solutions for you. I hope that as we discuss these together, I will make you laugh, think, perhaps even disagree; but at the end of the book you will feel a whole lot better.

More importantly, that you will see a path ahead that leads to sales success and all the things you have dreamt of in life.

Can you answer yes to any of the questions?

If so, this book is precisely for you.

Can I still sell?

Perhaps things have got to the point that you doubt your ability to sell successfully again. Maybe your confidence is low and you have lost that self-belief that made you successful in the first place.

Perhaps you are thinking seriously about a change of role because the going is too tough. Maybe I should move into Sales Administration? The old sales magic has gone; I'm too old, I've lost 'it'. There are younger people snapping at my heels who understand computers and technology far better than me.

Maybe now is the time to start taxi driving.

How can I improve my earnings?

You may have bought the book because you are desperate OR in a bid to improve already respectable levels of success. Either the credit cards are up to their maximum and you have to keep borrowing to pay the bills OR you would love to take that holiday of a lifetime next year and need to do better to achieve the earnings necessary. You need to turn things round quickly, but have no clear idea how reach your goal.

Sales dried up?

Perhaps you are in a business where you have been successful in the past, but sales have tailed off. You don't want to move to another market area – or indeed a different Company – but are asking "What do I have to do to turn things around?"

Maybe you have been on a recent Sales Course, only to come back more depressed than before, since everyone seems to have the answers except you!

How do I cope with all this regulation – and sell?

"I keep telling Management that my job is to sell, not administer. The lap-top was great when I first got it, but now I realise I'm doing more and more admin on it that used to be done by Head Office. It also goes wrong regularly and the support is not great. I have less time with customers and am ending up working 60 hour weeks on a regular basis.

If I have to fill in yet another new form telling them what I've already told them a dozen times before, I will explode. I'm fed up spending hours down-loading 105 page procedural manuals that come as attachments to an e-mail and clog up my machine."

New to Sales?

Are you keen to be the best you can be and outperform others' expectations?

Made redundant?

Perhaps you have just been 'downsized', laid off, re-structured, offered early retirement, or just plain fired. Maybe you are looking at a different market area in which to utilise your sales skills.

How can I reach Target?

They keep moving the goalposts and keep setting stiffer targets, in the mistaken belief that it is 'motivational'. I am doubtful of reaching this year's target and feel vulnerable.

I can't see an immediate end to this downturn. If only there was a bit of good news, something positive to hang on to. I know it's affecting my relationships: I'm getting ratty with the kids, blowing up for no reason at the check-out assistant at Tesco's. I've apologised more in the last 3 months than in the last three years for being irritable.

Why doesn't that Sales Manager get off my back?

OK, I know that she is also under pressure from the Board and so far our Regional Team has only hit 65% of Budget. Trouble is, she reckons we're just making excuses when we tell her that it's tough. She hasn't been at the sharp end for 20 years, so what does she know?

Why is my health getting worse?

I reckon it must be stress-related. I keep getting headaches, my neck and back are tense. I suspect my intake of alcohol is increasing. I wish I could smoke less. Sometimes I have a real churning in the stomach, especially before a meeting with Management.

I must get away for a holiday but can't afford it.

If you've answered yes to any of these questions,
you qualify to read this book.

I hope to challenge and inspire you as we walk through the chapters together: these are just words on a page, **but if you apply them and put these ideas into practice**, you will be successful.

Chapter Two

TOUGH TIMES

———————•◦✓◦•———————

We need to understand the 'big picture' in order to find the right answers. In sales, we operate in a particular time and place and this will have a major bearing on the strategy we employ for sales success. What worked in 1970 will not work in 2004.

The last few years have seen some momentous events: The Twin Towers (9/11), the Iraq War, collapse of Stock-Markets both in UK and US. Scandals have rocked the business world: WorldCom, Enron and the Equitable Life fiasco.

A few years before, we had the collapse of Lloyds of London and the demise of Baring's Bank, brought about by cheeky chappie Nick Leeson, now predictably a celebrity in his own right.

It's enough to make any sane salesman jump off the nearest cliff. The fact that you are reading this book indicates that thankfully you haven't taken this course of action. Like me, you believe there is real hope but are pragmatic enough to realise that times have changed and what worked 30 years ago will not work now.

Why are the British less positive than Americans?

If you are reading this in the UK, you are also aware of the grey smog of negativity that seems to envelop our green and pleasant land. It is still green and pleasant, although many of us seem to have forgotten that it is a good place to live; as Boris Johnson said in the Daily Telegraph recently, there is still a fundamental decency and honour in the British people.

If you are American, you will probably be more upbeat in spite of the wars and rumours of wars. The pioneering spirit that made America great is still alive, but 9/11 has left you as a nation crippled and bewildered.

Soon after the Twin Towers, it was reported in the US press that brokers on Wall Street, having lost colleagues in the carnage, were understandably allowing their emotions to affect their trading. Because they were feeling broken and upset by their loss, this led to a negative view of the markets, with resulting falls on the Dow Jones Index.

Entrepreneurial spirit

Sales magazines in the US are far more positive than comparable journals in the UK. As far as I'm aware, there are no comparable journals in the UK, which may be significant. There are Marketing magazines, but to my knowledge no monthly magazines devoted to Selling – perhaps we Brits deem it too vulgar!

In the US, Popular titles like 'Sales & Marketing Management' and 'Selling Power' offer intelligent, reasoned articles on beating the recession. Magazine articles in the UK on selling tend to major on the tired old 70s sales techniques.

In the US, *'Entrepreneur'* magazine and its sister magazine *'Be your own Boss'* offer hundreds of start up and franchise ideas, all infused with a sunny californian optimism, at least to my world-weary British eyes.

The very presence of these magazines in Barnes & Noble (the US equivalent of Waterstones) and other News-Stands across America gives the US salesman a lift: uplifting, positive messages to neutralise the bad news.

Why are things so difficult?

Let's get real, though. Times are tough. In virtually every business or profession, selling products or services is much more difficult than only 7 or 8 years ago. Why? In the UK, interest rates have been low for some years, the economy is in reasonable shape and the weather was pretty good for most of 2003.

There is something more going on than 'the glass is half-empty' standard response of the Brits. It is a crisis of confidence, especially in financial institutions.

The UK stockmarket has fallen over the past few years not primarily because of economic factors, but because of an erosion of confidence. Most of the money that should be in the equity markets is now in property, whether a main residence, buy-to-let in the UK or a villa in Spain which is part holiday home/part income generator.

Financial Advisers are finding that their clients are now investing in property funds, rather than equity funds as in the past 20 years.

The Englishman's home is his fortress

The Englishman's home has always been his castle: now it is his financial fortress against the uncertainties of post-modern Britain. House prices continue to defy gravity, home-owners are feverishly extending and improving their properties; the Government insists that more and more houses should be built on the postage stamp that is South East England.

So much of the money that 15 years ago was being spent by consumers on goods and services is being poured into bricks and mortar: that is a major reason that you are finding things difficult in your particular area of sales.

The Media strongly influences our Customers

In the UK, especially, we have to cope with a negative Press. It is difficult as salesmen not to be depressed – and hence de-motivated – by what we read. We are only human and no matter how hard we try to be cheerful and optimistic, smiling at every opportunity as instructed by sales text-books, wearing Daffy Duck ties to cheer ourselves up, it does get to us.

There is something both insidious and malicious about the British press – especially the tabloids – always on the look out for misery and bad news; delighting in wars, murder, crime, dishonesty, unfaithfulness; glorifying the excesses of the rich and famous, all in the name of investigative journalism, using self-righteous legitimation by the use of slogans like 'the public has a right to know'.

Why are we so cynical?

Glenn, a taxi driver friend of mine cites a good example of this. As you probably know, Sir Paul McCartney was the first to go over to the US straight after 9/11 and give his services free for a charity concert, wanting to show solidarity with a hurting nation. The ex-beatle has also recently undertaken gruelling world tours and patently doesn't need the money, being worth a cool £750 million.

Although a hero for his swift response in the States, the UK press murmured that he only did it for the money, the charity gig was to boost his popularity, etc. I don't believe a word of it. Our press have much to answer for.

Very few column inches are devoted to the thousands of stories every day of goodness, kindness, faithfulness and generosity. Newsreaders are laughed at if they have the temerity to suggest that reading out a bit more good news wouldn't go amiss.

The newspapers rarely print actual lies as such, because they know they can be sued: instead, they leave out chunks of the truth. Bad news sells newspapers, so why let the truth get in the way of a good story?

Enough. I am not playing moral watchdog but rather demonstrating what we are up against as salesmen. The Media is the backdrop to our lives and those of our clients. How our customers see the world is largely determined by its portrayal in the media and the world-view presented is largely negative.

Chapter Three

STARTERS
KNOWING ME, KNOWING YOU

Before you can understand others, you have to understand yourself. This may seem obvious, but it is striking that many sales people have little self-knowledge. Before you can sell to others, you have to understand them. Before you can understand them, you have to understand yourself.

Now I am not talking about years spent in therapy or long periods of introspection: rather, a working knowledge of what makes you tick is *essential* in successful selling.

You need to have a healthy self-awareness of your own strengths and weaknesses, especially emotional. Because the decision to buy on the part of the customer is essentially an emotional one, understanding your own emotions is a vital key to understanding the psychology of sales. Never undervalue the central role that emotions play in decision making.

People who don't 'know' themselves rarely make good salespeople, since they lack the sensitivity needed. You can observe them at parties, talking nineteen to the dozen, blissfully unaware of the effect they are having. The sort of people that think selling is all about talking as much as possible, when, as we shall explore later, 80% is listening.

Think back to the last major purchase you made. I am sure that you felt good, about yourself and life in general, when you took the decision. It is the same for our customers. They will often put off making a decision, because they don't feel right, often citing other reasons – 'I have to consult my daughter', 'I need more time', 'I need more information', etc.

Since men, especially, in British culture are not encouraged to express their feelings – Prince Charles would not make a good salesman – they are likely to be less aware of the feelings of others. This is starting to change with younger men.

What makes you tick?

Maybe you don't really know. Think very hard about why you get up in the morning and go to work. What drives you? Money, power, the desire to give good service,to provide for your family?

If it is money alone, you need to be careful. Customers instinctively know if you are driven purely by money, since this will manifest itself in being too pushy and directive – and will result in losing sales.

Customers can sense if you are putting your own needs above theirs. Short-term, you may be successful, but you will never build long term relationships and therefore repeat business which is the bedrock of sales success.

If it is money, be honest with yourself but resolve to change. Put the customer first and results will follow. As sales guru Zig Ziglar says *'The best way to get what you want is to help other people get what they want'*. It is a cliché, but 'look after your customers and they will look after you' is true. Indian Hotel magnate Raj Oberoi: *"Do the right job and money will surely follow"*.

How are you perceived by others?

I have asked a few clients I know really well and have sometimes been surprised by the answer. We almost invariably do not see ourselves as others see us and it is essential to know how we come across. We may think we are friendly and sociable, but if that comes across as smarmy we've lost the game.

I had a client who we shall call Mrs Hardwick back in the mid 1990's. A wealthy widow living in breezy Worthing, she invested around £20,000 with me over a period of four years. She mentioned vaguely that she had a sizeable Portfolio of other investments, but didn't volunteer any more information. I did regular annual reviews of her investments but it became clear that the relationship wasn't developing and so we lost touch. I was aware that we had never quite 'hit it off' and there was a nagging feeling at the back of my mind that I hadn't 'connected' with her.

Recently, Mrs Hardwick telephoned the Office, spoke to my wife Brenda (also an Independent Financial Adviser) to say she had some more money. Brenda went to see her and, in short, has invested in excess of £150,000 on her behalf. I asked Brenda to send Mrs Hardwick my regards and hoped she remembered me. She said yes, but gently mentioned that she found me a little, ahem, patronising and that 'I had an answer for everything'.

My suspicions were confirmed. I had blown it and wish I had mustered the courage to follow my hunches and ask the Client what was wrong. Being the usual considerate female, she had not volunteered these opinions, expecting no doubt that my ego was fragile, like most men.

Male salesmen need a far greater degree of sensitivity to female customers, an 'emotional radar' that will give us early warning signs if we are not hitting the right note. Don't do what I did: if in doubt, ask the customer if something is wrong. She will respect you for your honesty and that you are secure enough in yourself to be vulnerable. It's a myth that women like the 'me Tarzan, you Jane' approach and it certainly has no place in business.

Some salesmen think they have to 'act like salesmen', which involves speaking in a particular way, driving a specific car, dressing in a power suit. To a certain extent, it is true that all of us play different roles: salesman, father, friend and so on. Be yourself and allow your sales persona to be a natural extension of your own, unique personality.

We underestimate clients: they are not stupid and can usually spot a fake from 100 yards! Don't pretend to be someone you are not and resist the temptation to name-drop: it won't endear you to your customer. Similarly, driving an expensive car may have exactly the opposite effect on the customer to the one you intend. It may get their back up, knowing your car is better than theirs and they may think you are earning too much.

Know your own strengths and weaknesses

If you have a tendency to become angry or irritable, know the warning signs and either avoid a situation which triggers this off or withdraw before you get steamed up.

If you have driven 80 miles to see a customer and it is apparent that they are wasting your time, politely withdraw rather than get angry – although you will have vented your spleen, you'll regret it in the long run.

I believe it is a myth that allowing one's anger to overflow has a cathartic effect: in my experience, it has a corrosive quality and, more often than not, one would love to be able to turn back the clock.

Don't get angry

Anger has no place in selling and customers will forgive almost anything else, but not anger. Even if you apologise profusely afterwards, the damage is done.

We all respond differently to stress. Many books on selling go into detail about different personality types and how each type responds to stress. In a sales situation, the best antidote is to focus on the customer and his needs instead of your own. Stress can interfere in a big way with your ability to be objective; you need to understand intellectually what is happening, rather than allowing your emotions to dictate your response.

Don't react to the customer's stress

Don't take a client's anger or stress personally. Talk to yourself positively and remind yourself that the behaviour he is displaying is his way of coping. Don't copy his behaviour and respond out of your emotions – it is neither professional or appropriate

Take a deep breath, change the pace and if necessary, take a break to get yourself away from an 'intense' situation. The chances are that the client is also feeling uncomfortable and would welcome some respite. Regain perspective.

Maintain a healthy lifestyle

It amazes me how many salespeople pay little or no attention to their health. You can't have 36 beers, an explosive chicken vindaloo, steal a few guilty hours at a naughty lap-dancing club, pour yourself into a taxi at four in the morning and expect to make a superb client presentation five hours later. Alcohol does not relieve stress – it adds to it.

Especially amongst men in sales, there seems to be a macho attitude which legitimates excess and even encourages it.

Don't get me wrong: I'm not expecting that we'll be tucked up in bed at 9.30pm with a milky drink and an improving book. What I am saying is look after yourself, be professional – *it's your livelihood.*

Exercise is doubly important in an industry where stress can be the norm. The sales rep in the Company car, phone clamped to ear, negotiating a roundabout whilst eating a cheeseburger with one hand and reading a map with the other. I've seen it! Resist the temptation to 'relieve your stress' with a dose of the falling-down juice; take exercise instead.

If you are competitive, play to your strengths and take up a sport where you can be competitive and the exercise won't become a bore. If working out at the gym leaves you cold, try something else, but do something.

Know your best time of day

In a previous job as Sales Manager, I remember sharing an Office with one of the Consultants under my care. Trevor looked like an unmade bed. He wore shirts which he couldn't do up at the collar, drove a battered Ford Escort with ensuite dog, which he took everywhere because his wife didn't want to look after it. The interior of his car was like a council rubbish tip and he was invariably late. He was always asking me for advances of commission to pay off yet another credit card debt.

One Monday I was in the office with him all day. He made his first sales related telephone call at 4.47pm, having spent the previous 7 hours lighting cigarettes, answering personal correspondence, doing crosswords, poring over junk mail, lighting another cigarette, entering prize draws, feeding and watering the over-heated dog in the Ford Rubbish Tip, making endless cups of coffee, lighting another cigarette. You get the idea.

Although I'm not sure whether Trevor could ever have been successful, he would have stood a much better chance had he reversed the procedure: done the sales related activities first and left the rest until later. The chances are that he would then not have had time for all the other, sales-avoidance activities.

Many people are at their best in the mornings, so it makes sense to do the important tasks when you are at your best. In my early days in financial services, I spent two hours most mornings on the telephone making prospecting calls. If evenings are better for you, play to your strengths and make your phone calls then.

Much more about the use of the telephone in a later section.

Don't be too hard on yourself

We are all vulnerable human beings who don't always get things right. Bill Shankly once said of football *'it's not a matter of life and death – it's far more important than that'*. Although I know what he was trying to say, selling is not a matter of life and death. Get things in perspective. If you make a mistake, lose a large sale, even lose your job: it is not, repeat not, the end of the world.

There are some sales books I've read that tell you to live, eat and sleep sales if you want to be successful, that it needs to become your life. Tosh. The best salesmen have perspective: they see their lives as a whole, not broken down into compartments. They have a full life outside of their sales career and the stimulus this produces actually makes them more successful in selling.

Chapter Four

WHAT SKILLS ARE NEEDED TO BE A GREAT SALESMAN?

Selling is a people business. The oldest cliché in the book, but still an incisive truth with layers of meaning. Of course one needs the technical abilities required for a sales job – it would be difficult, for example, to be a musical instrument salesman without the musical ability to demonstrate the instruments – but essentially we are talking about inter-personal qualities.

A focus on technical skills, to the exclusion of human values, was all too evident in the financial services industry during the 80s and early 90s. John Clark in his excellent book *'The money or your life – re-uniting work and joy'* says *"Merchant banking and broking firms came to be dominated by young financial whizz-kids. No doubt about it, they were highly skilled. However, being expert as technicians but unrounded as humans, they lacked an ethical base."*

Feminine side

In the following chapters, we will be looking at the individual skills and qualities required for great salesmanship. If you have a sneak glance at them in advance, you will see a common theme emerging: sensitivity. Since the majority of salesmen are male, this may strike you as surprising. Surely traditional male attributes such as drive and assertiveness are needed. Yes, they are, but so-called feminine characteristics like intuition and empathy are just as important.

We have all had experience of poor salesmen, who would sell their grannies into slavery if it made them a sale. A cross between David Brent from BBC2's 'The Office' and Swiss Tony from 'The Fast Show', this twerp drinks Stella and tequila in copious quantities and drives too fast in a Japanese (cheaper than a BMW) coupé in startling red or shiny black, rear spoiler obligatory. All after-shave and wacky Looney Tunes ties. *(Serious note: don't ever wear a 'fun' tie in business if you want to be taken seriously.)*

These types make a lot of what sales managers term 'comfort calls' – appointments where forced bonhomie can run riot with companies or cronies who have no intention of buying from him. Thus he can always point to excellent activity levels on his call sheets.

The trouble is, clinically, the man is a zombie. He doesn't have a clue and nobody has ever had the heart – or the courage – to tell him so. Head stuffed full of outdated 70s sales techniques that you *do* to the customer to make him/her buy from you. All re-inforced by the obnoxious, hard-drinking, careless, six times divorced male colleagues he gets hopelessly drunk with at national company conventions where Bernard Manning is the star turn.

My caricature is a bit over the top, but you know what I mean. If only he would 'be himself' rather than try so hard to fit into the macho stereotype he might be successful. Only problem is, he doesn't know who he is, has none of the self-knowledge I referred to earlier as being vital in effective selling. For him the outward (Calvin Klein boxers, Oakleys, Ralph Lauren polo shirt) is far more important than what goes on inside, what makes him tick.

The culture he operates in militates against any hint of a 'feminine side', yet it is precisely those more feminine qualities that are needed.

Technical skills

During your sneak look at the next few chapter headings, you will also notice that I don't major on technical skills. Over the years, I've been regularly told by friends that a facility with figures must be the greatest factor in my success as a financial adviser. Sure, I need to know how to use a calculator correctly, but technical skills per se will never make someone a great – or even good – salesman.

John Clark again: *"One of the saddest phenomena in the professions these days is the doctor who doesn't know how to listen. Unable to establish a proper person-to-person relationship with the patient, the doctor focuses on the symptons and seeks to solve the problem entirely in technical terms. Alas, this phenomenon is not confined to doctors. The old-style family lawyer who knew the client as a person and who gave wise counsel, not merely technical help, is becoming rare too."*

I am taking for granted that you have the necessary technical skills to perform your sales job effectively; if you don't have them, clearly you need to acquire them. What do I mean by technical skills? In some ways it is easiest to explain when these skills are absent: obviously a Driving School Instructor who couldn't actually drive couldn't do the job. Assuming he could, whether he would be a good or great driving instructor would depend on the skills we discuss later.

Chapter Five

THE FORGOTTEN CUSTOMER
– PART ONE

In this section, I want to take you back over the past 50 years so that together we can understand how the Sales Market-Place has changed out of all recognition. This is not a trip down memory lane for the sake of it, but I hope it will yield valuable insights into Clients' expectations in the early 2000s.

Once we have identified those expectations, we can do our very best to give our Clients superb Customer Service, a theme which I am sure you will notice is woven into the fabric of this book.

We need to understand that legions of customers are operating with very different expectations of customer service from those actually responsible for giving it! *This is actually a profound subject in the context of this book and understanding it is a vital key to sales success, especially in tough times.*

The dramatic rise in consumer complaints across all industries and professions over the last 20 years is no accident: it is essentially a clash of expectations, with a dollop of the US litigation culture thrown in for good measure.

Customer Service in Crisis

I have a reproduction poster in my Office, dated 1946, showing the Man from the Pru, a dapper Noel Coward look-alike, opening the garden gate of the archetypal English country cottage. The whole scene radiates tranquility, order and harmony.

Before we disappear in a cloying celebration of nostalgia, let us consider the symbolism of the picture. For those over 60, this represents a lost world where, as Nancy Reagan memorably noted, *"you could tell the quality of a man by the shine of his shoes"*. Bunk. I am sure Robert Mugabe has shiny black shoes. And Saddam Hussein. However, I think I understand what Mrs Ex-President was hinting at. Outward appearances could be trusted; people and things were pretty much what they seemed.

Whether one agrees with Nancy's analysis is not the point. The 'grey' pound is very powerful and over the last 25 years, the corporate purchasing power of the retired has increased dramatically. This is a fact that companies and advertisers recognise – that vast wealth is in the hands of the sprightly and active retired, many of whom look ten years younger than their actual age. These mature citizens have vigour, aspirations and much better health than their ancestors; they also have much more money.

Most significantly, they do not think of themselves as old and still have unfulfilled aspirations and dreams. The paradigm of 40 years work then retirement, pipe, slippers and tending the garden is shifting. Advertisers are starting to understand this, which is why there is so much nostalgia woven into the fabric of TV, newspaper and magazine advertising.

Man and the Machine

Here we arrive at a major paradox of a rapidly changing Marketplace: Millions of affluent consumers hankering after old fashioned service and reliability, being sold to by a generation which is steeped in technology, e-commerce.... who do not question that they are 'slaves to the machine'; they don't even realise that they are.

This generation has grown up with the computer – as familiar a childhood companion as the teddy bear – and doesn't realise the incredible limitations of the binary system – you can have any answer, as long as it is yes or no. This has profound implications for business in that the Machine dictates terms to the user – and therefore their customers – and ends up being master rather than slave.

Because the computer can only deal in yes/no/on/off questions, it lacks virtually all of the abilities and skills required in selling. And yet, because public companies are, in the main, run by accountants who only see balance sheets and numbers, remorseless cost-cutting and downsizing (I love that phrase!) is rampant, despite public pronouncements that "Employees are our most valuable asset."

"I thought employees were supposed to be our most valuable assets, but apparently it's money..."

"..employees came in fifth... just behind paperclips."

This means – you've guessed it – that more and more functions best performed by human beings are handled by machines genetically ill-equipped to deal with them.

The customer, hankering after the Lost World of Noel Coward's Man from the Pru offering a face to face, unhurried human relationship is forced to put up with bewildering technology. If you are being burgled, press 3, if you are being assaulted, press 4 and try not to bleed over the telephone.

Tony the out of work Actor

Cue light classical music while your phone call is held in a virtual queue at an anonymous Call Centre in a Warehouse off the M25: you have just bought a Philips fax machine and can't make it work, you phone a Helpline number for their Technical Department and fondly imagine you're going to be put through to some seasoned old Brylcreemed engineer.

In reality, you are talking to Tony, a 27 year old actor with bleached hair, who's in-between jobs. He is not employed by Philips, but rather on a short term contract with a TeleMarketing Company. On the wall of the vast open-plan office hangs a sign that – depending on how you look at it – is either very depressing or highly exciting.

Under the words 'Calls handled since January', an electronic read-out is in constant motion. One minute the figure reads 323,987,542 – but look away for a minute and it's gone up by a hundred.

Is this customer service? Does Tony have any loyalty to Philips? Does it matter that customers know his Christian name (not his surname) but don't have a clue where Tony is geographically or who employs him? This is an operation which *processes* customers, hence the proud numbers on the sign, rather than **serving** them.

The prevailing mind-set is not customer focused, it is technology, systems driven, the result of a faceless accountant's remorseless drive for increased profitability, without the financial implications of having to employ all these Tonies. All their soft focus advertising, jingles telling us that they are "caring for you" and would rather die than have an unhappy customer, cannot disguise the truth: The ethos is driven by a Balance Sheet.

Customers are not fools. They realise that they are being fed false promises on Customer Service, especially by multinationals, proudly announcing *what they have no intention of delivering*. The Public knows, although they may not be able to articulate it, that their needs come a very poor second.

The Customer as Administrator

Try booking a ticket via the automated telephone service offered by Virgin Cinemas: *it takes technology 15 minutes to do what a human being could do in 30 seconds*. It is also a nerve-racking experience, since you have to get used to the disembodied, synthesised voice and press the correct buttons at exactly the right time and in the right sequence, fearful in the knowledge that one false move and you die – or at least have to abort and start the whole blessed rigmarole again.

Once more, you the Customer become the Do-It-Yourself Administrator for the Cinema, on an unpaid basis. You are obliged to obey the Machine's protocols, or you won't get a ticket, because there is no button marked 'please may I speak to a Human Being'. Crazy, isn't it?

The point is that the general expectation of the majority of the population is that commercial transactions should take place between human beings who know each other by name, *ie. have a relationship*. These are 'Old Market Place' customers, fed up with the tyranny of technology, who long to talk to a person.

Now please don't hear what I am not saying. I use technology in my own business as an Independent Financial Adviser – internet, fax, pc, e-mail, all the goodies – but usually have manual systems alongside, such as the good old fashioned client file, which will tell me whether Mr Trubshawe correctly completed a direct debit form on 25th January 1991. Now I may never need that information, but I can tell you from past experience that it will probably take an hour of frustrating researches to find out without the manual record.

A computer screen is a dreadful historian. I use a mobile phone – but only when I want to – so as to avoid situations like the Dad I saw the other day, taking a business call whilst trying to push his young daughter on the swings in the playground. When technology becomes our master to that extent, we really have lost the plot.

Little Chef Charm School

It's the same Do It Yourself philosophy at the Little Chef, where you pay £1.99 and are provided with the raw materials to make a toasted tea-cake, complete with those nasty individual wrapped pats of butter that grease your clothes so effectively.

When I had the audacity to suggest to the Name-Badge known as Jason-I-am-here-to-Serve-You that for two quid the teacake should be ready for consumption, he looked at me cunningly and pricelessly told me "customers prefer it that way".

Now, don't get me wrong – this total absence of a customer service concept is not the exclusive preserve of the young – far from it. There lurk thousands of middle-aged shopkeepers, the length and breadth of the land, who, like Basil Fawlty, patently failed their Charm School exams and detest interruptions, ie. Customers.

Human beings were not created to relate to machines. As I have sought to emphasise throughout, *relationships are absolutely crucial in selling*. It is vital that we place Customer Service in the 2000s into context; only then will we understand why Customer Service is in deep crisis.

Technology: Master or Slave?

Conscientious salespeople are repeatedly thwarted in their efforts to give good Customer Service because of the unyielding protocols imposed on them by inflexible computer systems. We cannot pretend that technology doesn't exist and neither should we want to, since technology can have many benefits.

Those salespeople that will really succeed today will have learnt to harness technology as their slave – not their master. They will have to cut a few corners to do their best for the customer, side-stepping stifling 'procedures' and ignoring red tape, doubtless earning the odd rap on the knuckles. But if they bring home the bacon in terms of increased profitability, management will overlook their administrative shortcomings.

Generation Gap

Not only does the customer want a face to face, one to one business relationship, but deep down so do the majority employed in customer services. It is remarkable how many with sales/service orientation, given even the smallest encouragement will, against all the odds, strive to give good service. It is all a question of attitude.

Recently, we were shoved from pillar to post by Britannic Assurance on a simple administrative query. After dealing with four separate, but equally obstructive and rude 'customer service' assistants, we were passed on to a helpful woman who solved the problem immediately. The difference? Her attitude. She wanted to help.

There are two major groups of people who do not share the same fundamental values regarding the nature of business relationships. An older generation with time on their hands, searching for a bygone age of Corner Shops, unhurried service and courtesy, who knew, by name, the bank managers, shopkeepers, butchers, bakers, candle-stick makers who used to serve them.

A younger generation used to speed, stress, balancing a mobile phone whilst negotiating a roundabout and eating a McDonalds.

You may feel I am spending too long on this analysis, but believe me it is essential to 'set the scene' before moving on to our 'Main Course'. *An understanding of how we got to where we are in Customer Service is vital for future sales success.*

Consumer Lobby

Over the last 40 years, another major sea-change has been the rise and rise of the Consumer Lobby. As with technology, we shall see that this has often had surprising, unintended and negative effects. Back in the 50s and 60s, by and large there was a fair degree of trust between advertisers/marketeers on the one hand, and the customer on the other.

In the UK, there is more scepticism than in the US about advertising: the American's stereotypical Englishman is a sceptical, downbeat individual, whilst the British have tended to see the Americans as gullible, optimistic and brash. In Britain we laugh easily at Homer Simpson's ready acceptance of any slogan that Duff Beer throws at him.

The 'Litigation Culture' – which we examine in more detail later – has changed all this. The customer has now become a consumer, with profound consequences for the fabric and structure of the sales process. Customers understood perfectly well the notion of caveat emptor (let the buyer beware) and purchased goods and services largely on the basis of trust and relationship with the vendor or salesman.

Consumers, on the other hand, tend to be pre-occupied with price and are very aware of their rights, enshrined in law. They know the cost of everything and the value of nothing.

As a consequence, they are not too bothered about establishing a relationship with the vendor, often preferring the impersonal nature of e-commerce and mail order. My mother was like this, perhaps because of her insular, Scots, Isle of Bute upbringing, and would go to great lengths to avoid human contact where possible in making her purchases.

When she once ventured into Dixon's to buy a TV set, she never understood that she couldn't have rock-bottom prices and delivery of the item ten minutes later by liveried chauffeur. I tried to explain that because of the knock-down price, the margins were not there for the store to offer much service; she believed I was being shifty and evasive in showing solidarity with the retailer.

Litigation Culture

The Litigation Culture, which drifted across the Atlantic from the States, is part of a wider societal shift which emphasises the rights of consumers and individuals, rather than their responsibilities as citizens. One of its fundamental tenets is that, if something goes wrong, there must be someone to blame. And, logically, someone to sue.

On a recent visit to the US, I casually picked up the Miami Yellow Pages. My eyes almost popped out of their sockets. There were 50 – yes 50 – pages of Law Firms and Attorneys, offering to represent you in lawsuits involving medical 'malpractice', stubbing your big toe on the Kool-Aid machine at work, almost anything involving normal human activity. The trouble is, though, you can't legislate against Life: in so many everyday situations, there is no culprit, no hero or villain – it's "just life".

This emphasis on rights has the subtle effect of shifting responsibility for an individual's actions onto someone else – be they an individual or an organisation. This leads to farcical episodes, reported in the national press, such as the IRA prisoner who sued the Prison for damages, caused by the stress that the poor dear endured whilst a riot was going on in a nearby Wing. His legal action was successful and the authorities coughed up the cash. Words fail me.

As salesmen, we are all affected by the litigation culture. If possible, though, don't allow yourself to get sucked into the 'covering your back' mentality: I know this can be easier said than done. Just remember that not every client is 'out to get you' – the vast majority still abide by the old maxim 'caveat emptor' and do understand that they are responsible for their actions.

Like so many things, the consumer lobby started off as a good thing, as an antidote to the rip-offs being perpetrated in businesses as disparate as used cars, financial services, double glazing, pyramid selling, to name but a few. Why anyone should want to buy a pyramid is beyond me, though – large and difficult to maintain.

It is ironic that the crisis in customer service has its roots in the very strength of the consumer lobby, which insists on seeing everybody as either consumer or producer, with the only relevant factor being cost. Because we have allowed the Consumer to become King and appoint Price as his Prince, companies are under incredible pressure to cut costs.

There is no such thing as a free lunch and the Consumer Lobby must realise they can't have it both ways. If you keep beating the vendor over the head with the stick of price, in a highly competitive market-place he will be forced to lower them. Large global corporations, with their economies of scale, can still afford to do this, but Customer Service **must** suffer as a result.

Service providers are only human and will be reluctant to establish relationships of trust with their customers, always looking over their shoulders, haunted by the spectre of possible legal action in the future. This is usually rendered possible by the Regulator's favourite analytical tool, hindsight.

The old fashioned corner shop can't compete on price. They may hang on to sufficient customers by dint of excellent, personal service, especially in affluent areas where customers are prepared to pay more to preserve a slice of Olde England or New England; alternatively, and more likely, they will sell up and the shop will re-incarnate as a branch of the sombre Alldays Chain, complete with grim-faced franchisee mentioned earlier. We have come, rather tidily, full circle. Our Alldays man, like his consumers....

Knows the cost of everything and the value of nothing.

Poisonous Regulation

First cousin to the Consumer Lobby and the Litigation Culture is the Regulatory Framework. Because, as we have seen, the consumer no longer trusts the vendor (and vice versa), vast regulatory frameworks have been erected around most businesses and professions, creating a culture of Enforcement.

Spectacular events like the demise of Lloyds of London, which brought bankruptcy to many, have hastened the process. Yes, there are rogues, but the way to eliminate them is not to bury the decent and honest with great steaming dollops of legislation, compliance and obligation.

Why is the teaching profession in such crisis? Because teachers' contracts of employment are documents of enforcement. The tasks which they used to (in the main) perform cheerfully, on a voluntary basis, are now part of their contract, in addition to the reams of paperwork which must be completed every time Justin thumps Jason in the playground.

Why are there so few new entrants to the world of financial services? Have you had a look at the Financial Services Authority Rule Book? If so, I'm surprised you haven't jumped off a cliff. No doubt financial advisers will soon have to fill in forms to document why they visited a Client's toilet, stating the nature and purpose of the visit; detailing the frequency, duration and precise nature of bowel movements (colour and texture, please) with a 'reason why' letter documenting why they didn't wash their hands. The lunatics are running the Asylum.

Big Brother

The fastest growing area in many professions and businesses is the Compliance or Regulatory Department: it is possible to earn a good salary frustrating the living daylights out of honest practitioners and thus preventing them from earning a living. OK, Compliance officers are only administering the law, someone has to do it, granted, in the same way as someone has to be a traffic warden.

My main gripe is not with Compliance/Regulatory staff as such, although choosing an occupation whose main purpose is negative bothers me a little. It is the skewed thinking behind the rules which is poisonous and should be resisted: The main thrust is that you are guilty: now prove your innocence.

Ofsted Inspectors in Education are often rude, gimlet-eyed failed teachers who delight in putting the fear of God into good, conscientious educators. It is now commonplace to hear of excellent, mature teachers leaving the profession in droves, as a result of the stress and sheer unfairness of preparing for and enduring an Ofsted inspection.

Chapter Six

MAIN COURSE
EMOTIONAL INTELLIGENCE IN SELLING

Armed with this brief analysis of Customer Service over the last 40 years, we can now get into the heart of what this book is all about. I use the word heart because great salesmen lead with their heart, not their head. Most customers make decisions to buy from the heart, and so it is not surprising that a deep understanding of the customer's emotions is vital.

Here and throughout the rest of the book, you will note that I take many examples from the financial services sector, as this is where I have spent the majority of my sales career. However, the same principles apply in every area of business and I'm sure you will be able to find parallels with your own selling environment.

Andrew Starke, features writer for FT's Investment Adviser magazine, notes that *"clients often only seek the services of a financial adviser during an emotional period in their lives. In all areas of sales, an emotional trigger is often the catalyst for making a buying decision."* Anna Bowes of national financial advice firm Chase de Vere: *"if a client is terribly nervous because something dreadful has just happened then you have to just wait for a more appropriate time. Client 'state-of mind' is one of the most important areas to consider."*

What is Emotional Intelligence?

One of the best definitions I have come across is from best-selling high priest of Emotional Intelligence, Daniel Goleman, based on research done whilst at Harvard:

"The rules for work are changing. They take for granted intellectual ability and technical know-how. Instead, they focus on personal qualities, such as empathy, initiative, adaptability and persuasiveness. This is no passing fad: the data that argue for taking it seriously are based on studies of tens of thousands of working people."

These ideas are not new to the work-place; how people manage themselves and relate to those around them is central to much classic sales and management theory. What's new is the data: there are 25 years' worth of empirical studies that tell us, with real precision, that emotional intelligence is vital for sales success. Understandably, you may be sceptical of a subject which perhaps you associate more with faddish, 'pop' psychology, but believe me, this is centrally important.

If someone lacks emotional intelligence, it is usually obvious and the results can be disastrous. I play club cricket on a Sunday and a few years ago one of our team broke a finger attempting a catch, just prior to the end of the match. Our captain, ex-RAF, nice chap but rather rigid of mind-set, insisted, soon after the injury, on asking this guy, who was in a lot of pain, blood gushing from finger, whether he was available for next week's game.

You see, straight after the game was when he always asked people about their availability and he couldn't adapt to a different situation: a lack of emotional intelligence. We would never do that, you say, but I see this sort of thing happening all the time in sales situations.

If we are pre-occupied with our own agenda and train of thought, we will miss so many important 'cues' from customers and wonder why we are unsuccessful. We need to be able to 'read' people. Although no fan of mind-readers and fortune-tellers, they are often successful because of their intuitive ability to tell their customers what they want to hear!

Some common misconceptions

Emotional intelligence does not mean merely 'being nice', nor does it mean giving free rein to feelings – 'letting it all hang out'. Rather it means managing feelings so that they are expressed effectively and appropriately.

Nor are women 'smarter' than men in this department, although it is true that women are more aware, on average, of their emotions, show more empathy and are more adept interpersonally (from a study of thousands of men and women in 1997 by Reuven Bar-On, Toronto). Men, on the other hand, tend to be more confident, adaptable, optimistic and handle stress better.

In general, though, there are far more similarities than differences. Also, our level of emotional intelligence is not fixed genetically and, unlike IQ, which doesn't really change after teenage years, E.I. continues to develop with life's experiences.

Studies have shown that, over the years, people get better in this key skill as they grow more adept at handling their own emotions and refining their empathy and social skills. There is an old-fashioned word for this growth in emotional intelligence: maturity.

I have outlined below a framework for looking at the subject in greater detail:

- **Self-awareness**
- **Self-management**
- **Motivation**
- **Empathy**
- **Social Skills**

The first three topics relate to how we manage ourselves and the latter two, how we handle relationships.

Chapter Seven

SELF-AWARENESS

Before we look at the inside of the salesman, let's take a look at the outside. First impressions are important and during the first 30 seconds of a meeting, potential clients are subconsciously forming a judgement about you. As well as non-verbal clues such as body language, your appearance says a lot about you. Women are usually more aware of this than men, knowing that in business they will often be judged on how they look.

Although a generalisation, men are not so bothered – look at any Cabinet photograph in the 1970s and you will see what I mean. Michael Foot, the 'eminence grise' of the labour party, for all his obvious integrity, was never going to be successful in his duffle coat and wild 'Gone with the wind' hair.

Tory grandee Cecil Parkinson, on the other hand – not perhaps noted for his moral rectitude – always looked the part and was far more successful. Like it or not, presentation really matters.

Being male, I can only talk with any knowledge about presentation for men. Here are a few thoughts:

● You gets what you pay for, guv'nor. A cheap suit looks what it is – cheap. Three good suits are worth six mediocre outfits, so pay the maximum you can afford on this most basic item of male business wear. You will spend most of your working life in suits and as a sales professional you want to be associated with quality in your customer's mind.

● It'll ride up with wear. Oh no it won't. The old cliché is bunk. If it doesn't fit, get it altered. If you can't get it altered, chuck it away and start again.

Sorry, but your customers will notice that your shirt doesn't do up at the neck properly because you have put on weight. They will notice that your trousers are too short and make you look mildly amusing. They will notice the unattractive expanse of white leg showing above the sock, because of afore-mentioned trousers.

● You can tell a man by the shine on his shoes.

Keep your shoes (not loafers or boots) clean and make sure the chewing gum is removed from the soles.

● Don't play it for laughs. Resist the temptation to wear a Daffy Duck tie – even if your 9 year-old son has bought it for you and will be upset if you don't wear it. The same goes for Homer Simpson cuff-links and any other outward 'fun' item of clobber.

● Ask for help. If you are not sure about what to wear, ask someone else – probably female. If you are too embarrassed to ask, buy a book like 'Gentleman' by Bernard Roetzel, published by Konemann; this is an excellent guide to style and good taste in dressing for business.

Having looked at self-awareness on the outside, we now need to turn our attention to the inner aspects.

What is Self-awareness?

Why is it so important? Because successful selling comes from the **inside**, not from a series of external techniques learnt on a training course. At this point you might say "but Laurie, I am too busy trying to earn a living to have time to indulge in this psycho-babble." That statement, in a nutshell, encapsulates so much of what is wrong with 21st century Western society. *We are all too busy.*

We are all too busy because living in the West is expensive and we need to earn a good living to service the mortgage, pay for the car, holidays – the list is endless. That is all true, but what is not true is that money per se will bring us the happiness we desperately crave: that is quite clear from the lives of the rich, famous and miserable.

Also, in the West we have the notion that happiness is a *right*: try telling that to a slum-dweller in Bombay. I have seen villagers in India happy and contented, earning 100 rupees a day (about £1.35) so money can't be the secret. Having a purpose in life brings fulfilment and I would suggest that in selling that purpose should be serving the client/customer; if we do this, the rewards will surely follow.

I suggest that we take some time to look at ourselves, not in an introspective, navel-gazing way, but positively, constructively, to see what actually makes us tick. That is the beginning of self-awareness!

Cold showers

Self-awareness is knowing what makes us tick. Men can sometimes find this subject embarrassing, whilst women are generally more comfortable with it, since they often have greater self-understanding.

If you don't believe me, just look at the older male members of our royal family. The Duke of Edinburgh, Prince Philip must be one of the least self-aware men ever, otherwise he couldn't have come out with some of his immortal gaffes. A childhood of emotional frozen-ness, cold showers and distant parents gave birth to a man seemingly incapable of self-knowledge.

From 'The Tact and Diplomacy of Prince Philip' on the Internet: 'In 1993, the Duke comforted the residents of Lockerbie (the airplane disaster that killed hundreds) by telling them "People usually say that after a fire it is water damage that is the worst. We are still trying to dry out Windsor Castle."

But the Duke's affinity with the common people extends far beyond the UK. During a trip to Canada he said "we don't come here for our health. We can think of other ways of enjoying ourselves."

It is well known that Prince Philip has always been frustrated in his role as the Queen's consort, always one pace behind Her Majesty; it is no secret that he has always wanted to carve out a role for himself, in his own right, on the world stage. He has failed largely through a lack of self-awareness.

Why is Self-awareness so important in Selling?

Because self-awareness is a commercial asset, quantifiable in terms of profit like other skills and abilities. That can be seen from the examples of my failure with Mrs Hardwick, and Prince Philip.

Because good salesmen work intuitively, know how to manage themselves effectively and know how important the inner life of the salesman is. They know how they come across to others, having been teachable during their working lives, sensitive but responsive to constructive criticism.

Remember back to the anecdote about Mrs Hardwick earlier. I could have dismissed her comments about me being patronising, but I knew she was right and resolved to change my behaviour. Becoming more self-aware has therefore resulted in more sales to female clients and more income.

Let us look at Self-awareness under three headings:

Who am I?: Recognising your emotions and their effects.

Being honest with yourself: Knowing your strengths and weaknesses.

Self-confidence: a sense of self-esteem and one's own capabilities.

Chapter Eight

WHO AM I?

―――――――**●❤●**―――――――

We laugh at Alan Partridge, the half-failed, naffly dressed Norwich disc-jockey portrayed so incisively by Steve Coogan on British TV. 'Knowing me, knowing you' is his catch-phrase but it is obvious from his complete lack of sensitivity that he neither knows himself, nor anyone else. Partridge doesn't understand his own emotions or their effects, otherwise he could never have said to his long-suffering P.A. "technically, Lyn, your life isn't worth insuring."

We laugh at Partridge because we recognise in him so many others we know that are like him, ie. totally lacking in self-awareness. Do we recognise anything of ourself in him?

We ignore our emotions at our peril. I read of a Doctor who was offered a business proposition. If he would leave his practice to become medical director of a start-up health resort and invest £75,000 of his own money, the business plan projected that he would make a profit of £3 million within 3 years. He went ahead, sold his medical practice and invested in the resort.

But during the start-up year he found that there was no medical programme to direct yet – essentially, he spent his days as a salesman, trying to sell people time-shares in the resort. He went bankrupt within a few years.

At the outset, he had a gut feeling that there was something wrong with the proposition, that the projections in the business plan were too optimistic; however he craved change and the financial incentives clouded his judgment: he fatally ignored his emotions.

Of 60 highly successful entrepreneurs connected with companies with revenues between $2 million to $400 million, only one said his business decisions were made using the classic 'decision-tree' method, ie. purely rationally. The other 59 all said they used their feelings to confirm (or not) a rational analysis or let their emotions guide them at the outset and subsequently looked for data or a rationale that supported their gut feeling, or 'hunch'.

The Virgin King

It is clear from Richard Branson's autobiography 'Losing my Virginity' that he never set out with a grand master design to create a global brand. 17 year old Branson launched 'Student' magazine from a telephone box with a £4 loan from his mother: it became highly successful and was the launch-pad for what eventually became the Virgin Empire. In 1992 he sold Virgin Music – a part of that empire – for £510 million to Thorn EMI. He is now a billionaire.

Although a brilliant negotiator, superb entrepreneur and fearsome opponent – as British Airways' Lord King found out, to his cost (and subsequent resignation) – it is clear that Branson's business decisions were based more on feelings and intuition than cold logic.

Tim Jackson's biography 'Virgin King' makes the point that Branson has a high degree of self-knowledge and his people skills are apparent in the way he treats his staff. Jackson: *"His company is one of the least hierarchical one could come across. Branson pays as much attention to a chat with a post-room clerk as to a memo from his marketing director. It is no accident that Penni Pike, his senior P.A., has been with him since 1977."*

People who are self-aware:

● Know which emotions they are feeling and why.

● Realise the connections between their feelings and what they think, do and say.

● Recognise how their feelings affect their performance.

● Have a guiding awareness of their values and goals.

Tune in to feelings

The awareness of how our emotions affect what we are doing is the fundamental emotional skill. Such awareness is crucial in tuning in with accuracy to the feelings of our customers and colleagues. It is no surprise that outstanding counsellors and therapists display this skill to a marked degree.

This skill is vital to sales success, and at American Express, financial advisers' awareness of their own emotions is a competence central to excellent sales performance. Kate Cannon, Director of Leadership Development at the Company: *"The interaction between the client and an Adviser is delicate, dealing not only with hard questions about money, but also when the subject of life assurance comes up, the more sensitive issue of mortality."*

Often the Company found that Clients displayed feelings of distress, distrust and uneasiness, emotions that were all too often ignored by Advisers in their haste to make a sale.

American Express realised that they would have to train their Advisers to 'tune in' to this sea of feeling and handle it effectively in order to better serve their Clients. Notice again, the use of the word 'serve': many companies go through the motions of putting the customer first, stating that they really care for the Customer, pretending that they are actually in business to offer pastoral care and social work-type services!

Phrases like 'Customer Care' and 'Relationship Manager' are popular, but so often large companies say one thing in their advertising, but do something completely different. The reality – especially in the area of administration – is often a complete shambles. Back to the plot.

Emotional awareness starts with tuning in to the stream of feeling within us and recognising how our emotions mould how we think, perceive and act. From this awareness comes another – that our feelings affect those we deal with. As we have seen before, lack of this awareness can have really negative consequences, especially if we are not in touch with those feelings.

George W. Bush : *"The problem with the French is that they don't have a word for entrepreneur."* (I include this not because it demonstrates my point, but because I just love the quote. Sorry.) The next gem does demonstrate my point, however: *"We are fully committed to working with both sides to bring terror down to an acceptable level for both."* ('Dubya' after a meeting with congressional leaders in Washington, 2002).

I am sure that the President's comments will have given both the Israelis and the Palestinians renewed hope and done much to reassure the bereaved of both nations, secure in the knowledge that terror was to be reduced to an *acceptable* level. A little insensitive, perhaps?

You may have watched Terry Wogan during one of his chat shows and been tempted to remark "oh that's so easy, even I could do it." Wogan has the knack of making a very difficult job look simple and Cambridge University's 'Footlights' Dramatic Society's motto 'The Art is to conceal the Art' applies readily to the genial Irishman.

One of the secrets is that Wogan knows himself inside out and uses his own emotions and feelings to great effect during interview situations. He has a precise awareness of how he is coming across to his celebrity guests and will utilise his feelings to get the most out of them. Yes, he has an easy Irish charm which bewitches people, but underneath this is a powerful, incisive intelligence, combined with highly-developed, intuitive skills. To use our selling jargon, 'he is in touch with his feminine side'.

An Actor's Life for me

Great actors are vitally in touch with their emotions and it is this which produces great performances. Remember I said a few pages ago that Self-Awareness means not only being aware of our feelings but also their *effects* – on others.

Hugh Morrison, Staff Director at RADA says *"a good, mature actor whose personality is stable will be well aware already of the strength and weakness of his emotions."* Mediocre actors, on the other hand, come across as wooden and the layman, without any formal drama training, will instinctively know that the performance does not come from the heart.

Morrison goes on to say of a tense actor *"he is looking for what he cannot find, since by his tension he is blocking emotion and clear thinking."* What has this got to do with selling, you might ask? A great deal, because both professions require the same skills: an actor is ineffective when his emotions are blocked, unable to think clearly: so is the salesman.

Notice that Morrison mentions that when we are tense, we are unable to think clearly, because our emotions are clouding our thought processes.

If you and I think back to some of our worst sales presentations, we will often talk in terms such as 'I wasn't feeling right or I was uptight because I was late, feeling stressed because I had forgotten a vital item of sales literature, etc.' Feelings, feelings, feelings.

How to overcome negative feelings

The first step to overcoming these negative feelings is to recognise them accurately and then to take action: either, to manage our feelings effectively, so that they don't affect our performance, or if we are really finding this difficult, to withdraw from the situation altogether and arrange an alternative appointment.

Paulo Coelho is the Brazilian author of 'The Alchemist', a novel which has sold over 20 million copies world-wide. The book's sleeve notes say 'this is a transforming novel about the essential wisdom of following our dreams and listening to our hearts.' This is another way of saying that we must be in touch with our feelings if we are to fully develop into the very best we can be in our chosen career or profession, to truly fulfil our destiny.

Now I'm not suggesting that we all start part-time courses in Performing Arts, although it would probably help our sales skills. I am trying to help us not to see things in compartments, but that the skills required in acting – being aware of our feelings and their effects on others – are the same as in selling.

In a sense, in any sales situation we are putting on a performance. I don't mean that we are in some way being false and pretending to be someone we are not, but rather that, as with a stage performance, the adrenalin is going and we are presenting a particular persona to the customer. Perhaps it is no surprise, therefore, that many actors who are 'resting' (ie. between acting engagements) are taken on in sales jobs!

You are reading this book because you want sales success in tough times. Can I encourage you to read more widely, not just standard text-books on sales and motivation? I have come across profound insights into the sales process from reading works as diverse as Sting's biography, the Bible and the poems of William Blake.

We are all human beings who share the same emotions and what works in one sphere of life is transferable into another. The best salesmen are often well-rounded human beings with an endless curiosity about life in all its diversity, whose reading, listening and viewing enriches their working lives and makes them better at their job.

Take time to engage our feelings

With the frantic pace of life in the West, it is difficult to be self-aware. Please remember that, again, I do not mean being introspective: I am talking about a positive, healthy self-awareness. In the rush and pressure of the working day, our minds are pre-occupied with a stream of thought – planning the next thing, immersion in our current task, the knowledge of things not yet done tugging at our sleeve mentally.

It takes a deliberate mental pause to become sensitive to the emotional backdrop of our feelings, which we rarely do. Our feelings are always there, but we are seldom conscious of them. Instead, we typically become aware of our emotions only when they build up and boil over, usually in a negative way.

The pace and rhythms of life in 21st century give us little time to assimilate, reflect and respond. Our bodies are geared to a slower rhythm. Our rushed lives silence our emotions, but they are still rumbling on and are pushed into the subconscious.

This mental pressure dampens down the quiet inner voice which should be our guide and it is clear that people who are out of touch with their feelings are at a tremendous disadvantage. In a sense, they are 'emotional illiterates' who are unaware of a whole dimension of life which is crucial for success in life, let alone work.

For some, this emotional 'tone deafness' takes the form of total unawareness (or deliberate ignoring) of the messages their bodies are sending them – in the guise of chronic headaches, back pain, anxiety attacks, stress.

At the other extreme, we have all met people with no awareness of the feelings of others and suppression – or little understanding – of their own. The correct term for such people who function within the boundaries of honest society is 'sociopath'; those who function outside the boundaries and whose anti-social personalities result in crime are called pyschopaths.

One can easily reel off a list of the usual suspects who are examples of the latter: Saddam Hussein, Idi Amin, Kray Twins to name but a few from a most unpleasant bunch. I am sure we have all met individuals – particularly on the roads of Britain – who fall into the first category, hopefully not the second!

Because sociopaths have little understanding of their own emotions and do not realise that others have different feelings, my observation has been that they view their own emotions and desires as being the guiding factor, the arbiter in any situation.

The cuddly Marquis de Sade based his philosophy on this maxim, as did the rather nasty Aleister Crowley. Rock star Marilyn Manson would be a more recent example of a trainee sociopath. As far as they are/were concerned, their feelings – no matter how damaging and inappropriate – are correct and logical and therefore they don't expect others to question their actions.

Have fun improving your Self-awareness

The good news is that self-awareness is a skill that can be nurtured and developed – as long as one is just sufficiently self-aware to realise that this is an area of weakness. It takes time. Five minutes per month set aside to become more self-aware just will not work.

I have been learning the piano over the last few years and have found it a very real help in unlocking feelings and giving me space to reflect. Just having a weekly piano lesson in a totally different, non-work environment has been incredibly helpful, as have my thrice-weekly half hour practice sessions. Hopefully, I will end up the most self-aware musician that ever lived.

Don't be silly Laurie, you don't understand, I just don't have time for the luxury of taking time out. Yes, you do and without me getting side-tracked into a chapter on time management, you owe it to yourself to make time. This is so important to your mental well-being that it is essential that you programme into your diary regular activities, which you really enjoy, outside of work.

The important thing is that whatever you choose must be something you really enjoy, rather than a chore to be endured.

I tried the gym for nine months, hated every moment of it and now play badminton instead – great exercise and an outlet for my natural competitiveness.

As we pass on to the second part of this section, I hope I have demonstrated that, rather than psycho-babble, self-awareness is vital for sales success.

Chapter Nine

BEING HONEST
WITH YOURSELF

A s I take you on this journey through the salesman's psyche, I hope you are not finding it too harrowing. If you need a gin and tonic and a lie-down in a dark room, I will understand.

I hope that you are starting to see that Emotional Intelligence is one of the strongest weapons in the Salesman's armoury, far more potent than any number of 'closing techniques'. Yes, I do appreciate that one needs to have the self-confidence to 'ask for the order', but it doesn't matter how many closing techniques you have learnt, if you lack the self-confidence to deliver them!

If I have unwittingly demolished such self-confidence as you already possessed, please don't worry- help is at hand in a later section on this very subject.

I trust you are now feeling better after your lie-down. Let us move on to look at a vital aspect of self-awareness: Being honest with yourself.

Please ignore any mental pictures of a psychiatrist's couch and a 'Shrink' asking you to interpret ink-blots. By now, I hope you know me well enough to realise that I am not going to bang on about introspective self-analysis.

Don't get me wrong – therapy can be very helpful – but this is essentially a book designed to help you achieve *commercial* success. Being honest with yourself is a preliminary to increasing your self-confidence and that is why we will tackle the former subject first.

Being honest with ourselves is not easy, but it is a vital preliminary to knowing our strengths and weaknesses. My friends tell me that one of my few better qualities is the ability to acknowledge my shortcomings. I'm proud of being humble. However, I would have to say that, to some extent, it is a self-defence mechanism: I have found in life that if you are not honest with yourself, someone else will be, and probably a lot less politely.

I don't understand the likes of Jeffrey Archer who lie through their teeth, because self-interest alone would dictate that you own up, since it usually results in a shorter prison sentence. *One of the great things about telling the truth is you don't have to remember what you said.*

Before I get carried away on the moral high-ground, if I can't appeal to your higher nature, let me urge you on the grounds of naked self-interest to develop the habit of being honest with yourself.

The effects are very positive, as I observe with my son Sam. If he has done something wrong, he will draw my attention to it immediately, in a self-deprecating way – and it always meets with a lesser reaction on my part than if he'd been secretive and I discovered it for myself. Maybe he has learnt this from me, but the net result is that his honesty gets him out of trouble.

Self-knowledge is a commercial asset

Being honest with ourselves is vital in accurately assessing our strengths and weaknesses. This is important in the hard-nosed world of commerce and remember this book is all about sales success, not some airy-fairy Neverland where we feel better but it has no impact on our income.

Rob Goffee and Gareth Jones, in their excellent article in a recent Financial Times Supplement titled Mastering Leadership, state that *"many executives don't have the self-knowledge for leadership. Our work suggests that the most effective leaders share four rather unexpected characteristics. The first is that leaders reveal their weaknesses. Great leaders acknowledge their incompleteness – they even make it work for them."*

Perhaps some of these ideas are new to you. Maybe you are getting exasperated with me, wondering when I'll get to the meaty Close that Sale bits, sledgehammer 'power phrases' that compel the client to buy: secretly thinking that Mellor has to pad it out to justify the cover price. Nothing could be further from the truth.

Remember I said elsewhere that so much of traditional sales training concentrates on the outside of the salesman, ignoring the far more important inner aspects. If you still don't believe me, have a look at the following case study.

Mort Meyerson, Chief Executive Officer of US computer services company Perot Systems, wrote a surprisingly revealing and introspective article titled 'Everything I thought I knew about leadership was wrong', shortly after joining Perot.

Even the title of the piece shows the honesty of the man. Previously CEO at computer services giant EDS, within the first six months in his new job, he realised that, compared to the organisational world he was used to at EDS, everything had changed. The technology, the customers and the market – but also the people who worked for him and their reasons for working.

Meyerson went through a time of intense self-examination, wrestling with questions that went to the heart of the leadership style he had prided himself on. He came to see that during his years at EDS, he had been both very successful and very ruthless.

In looking back, though, he also saw that he had created immense personal misery for his employees even as he made them rich. At EDS, eighty-hour working weeks were routine, employees were moved from location to location without a second's thought for their welfare and the disruption it might cause them and their families.

One day, despite a very heavy snowfall, every member of the team managed to get to work – except one, Max Hopper.

Meyerson was furious and shouted at him with the result that Hopper left EDS at the earliest opportunity – and went on to revolutionise the airline reservation industry by inventing the Sabre computerised system.

Reflecting on his alienation of Hopper, a superbly talented employee, Meyerson admitted he was far too quick to make harsh judgments and too slow to see the other person's point of view. He came to realise that what he had considered strengths were now more clearly identified as weaknesses.

He started to understand that today a leader needs to be receptive to honest, direct messages from anywhere and everywhere in a company. He changed. Having been honest, he began to identify his strengths and weaknesses. He set up an e-mail address and received thousands of messages per month, all of which he read. He even sent a congratulatory e-mail to a team who made a great sale, within an hour of their victory.

Joe Jaworski, formerly with Royal Dutch/Shell's scenario planning group: *"Before you can lead others, before you can help others, you have to discover yourself."* We can see, then, that being honest with ourself is a vital pre-requisite to knowing our strengths and weaknesses. If we can enhance our strengths and minimise our weaknesses, we will be more successful and earn more.

Robert E. Kaplan, in his book *'Beyond Ambition'* identifies some of the more common weaknesses – or blind spots – which can prevent us achieving our goals and fulfilling the potential within:

Unrealistic goals: Setting overly ambitious, unattainable goals, perhaps at the prompting of Management, is a recipe for frustration and disillusionment! Someone once said that you usually achieve much less than you expect in the first two years in sales, but far more in five. 'By the yard, it's hard; by the inch, it's a cinch' is an oft-quoted phrase in selling. It's far better to set realistic goals broken down into bite-size chunks.

Relentless striving: Compulsively hard-working at the expense of all else in life; 'running on empty' can lead to burnout and health problems.

Driving others: Pushing others – work colleagues and family – too hard, burning them out; coming across as abrasive or ruthless, insensitive to the emotional harm to others.

Ambition: Not necessarily a bad quality in itself, although 'blind' ambition often means that we have to win at all costs, competing instead of co-operating; being boastful and arrogant; seeing people as allies or enemies in black and white terms.

Pre-occupation with appearances: Needing to look good at all times; overly concerned with public image; craving the material trappings of high income.

Needing to appear perfect: Enraged by or rejecting criticism, even if accurate and honest; blaming others for his/her failures; cannot admit mistakes or personal weaknesses.

How can we improve?

It's a pretty horrible list and if we're honest we can probably spot ourself in there somewhere. But there is hope. As Daniel Goleman says *"all work-place competencies are learned habits" – if we are deficient in one or another, we can learn to do better. The arrogant and impatient person can learn to listen; the workaholic can slow down and find more balance in life.*

But those improvements will never happen without the first step, which is to become aware of how these habits damage us and poison our relationships. As the Head of Executive Development at a Fortune 500 company told me 'the biggest problem around here is the lack of self-awareness'."

Being teachable

Being teachable is one of the most vital keys to unlocking our sales potential and opening up a treasure chest of possibilities we never imagined. It is a choice, not a feeling, and it requires humility.

Star performers intentionally seek out feedback; they want to hear how others perceive them and are secure enough to handle it. Graham Gooch, one of England's best post-war batsmen, often asked for advice and help from his colleagues, cricketers far less able than him.

Find people close to you that you really trust and ask them to be honest with you about your strengths and weaknesses. Although you may not like their answers, if you can swallow hard and embrace the necessary changes, so much of your true potential will be released.

Chapter Ten

SELF-CONFIDENCE

Self-confidence is not the same as arrogance. Now I am sure you already know that, but when someone who is fundamentally insecure is encouraged to be self-confident, it often manifests itself as arrogance.

Insecurity – the mother of arrogance

I have met scores of people in business – usually men – who have to massage their egos in conversation to boost their fragile self-confidence. They are too quick to give you their business card. Why? To demonstrate their self-importance, masking insecurity.

Think back to social situations you have been in. Perhaps a party, where you are introduced to someone new: they tell you about (a) their new car (b) their fantastic job (c) their distant connection with royalty; what comes across is not confidence, but arrogance, and the root of it is insecurity.

Take singer Robbie Williams, for example. Yes, he has bags of talent, but is also massively insecure which manifests itself in a 'look at how good I am' stage presence. Propped up by drugs, alcohol and a lifestyle Ann Widdecombe would certainly disapprove of, he admitted recently that *"the only way I cope with a bad press is by realising that I know worse things about myself than they do"*.

Arrogance in a public figure like Williams is almost encouraged by his fans, but in a face to face sales situation, it will lose you sales and income. The impression a customer will get, being on the receiving end, is of a salesman who never stops talking about himself and who therefore has little interest in the customer or his needs.

Selling is 80% listening/20% talking

We are all insecure, to a greater or lesser extent, but the good news is that self-confidence can be developed and strengthened. Again, though, it requires courage to enable us to be honest with ourselves, humble enough to face up to the fact that we are all Forrest Gumps.

Have you ever wondered why people may always seem to be in a hurry to get somewhere else, looking at their watch, when you want to chat? In the Good Book it says *'the truth will set you free'* and facing up to the truth about ourselves will also set us free. If we have the courage to face up to our shortcomings, we are at least 80% of the way to over–coming them!

Now, having outlined what self- confidence is not, let us move on to discuss what it is. People that are self-confident:

● Present themselves with self-assurance....
  but not arrogance.

● Have what is termed 'presence'.

● Can voice views that are unpopular and go out on a limb for what they believe is right.

- Are decisive, able to make sound decisions, despite pressures and uncertainties.

- Win others to their point of view by persuasion, not bullying.

- Use their charm and excellent inter-personal skills to win the argument. Charm is not the same as smarm or creeping and people know the difference!

- Make others feel good and are sought out as friends.

This list is by no means exhaustive, but I am describing someone that either your or me would like to be. The individual described is attractive and would clearly be a hit at parties. In a business situation, he or she is a winner.

Courage of his convictions

Let me tell you a true story about an executive who was brought in to head up a privately owned airline in a small Latin American country. He found the business in a total mess, falling revenues the result of favouritism and 'jobs for the boys'. The main sales agent for the airline was a close friend of the owner, and his contract was far more favourable than his main competitor's, and yet his agency was a weak performer sales-wise.

The contracts for the pilots were excessively generous and they belonged to one of the most powerful unions in the country. These contracts were a major drain on the Company's balance sheet and pay was far above the industry standard.

People warned the new executive not to take on the unions; people who did sometimes found their own lives in danger or their family threatened. Such was the new man's self-confidence that he confronted the problems head on. He told the pilots that the Company would be bankrupted if they didn't lower their pay expectations. The pilots listened and increased their working hours without demanding more money.

Buoyed by this first success, our hero asked for an interview with the owner, stating directly that the owner's close friend, boss of the ticket agency mentioned before, was incompetent and wasn't producing the goods revenue-wise. "Get rid of that agency or I am leaving", he said. The owner listened and cancelled his crony's contract.

As a friend of the brave executive put it "he was willing to confront even when his own job and personal safety were at stake." Such self-confidence is the foundation for outstanding success – in general business management, or sales. Without it, people lack the conviction that is essential for taking on tough challenges. In the current economic climate, it is an absolute pre-requisite to sales success, especially in the financial and service sectors.

For those who lack this quality, every failure confirms and re-inforces a sense of incompetence. The absence of self-confidence can manifest itself in feelings of powerlessness, helplessness and crippling self-doubt.

In the one-to-one sales coaching sessions I undertake, I have found that lack of self-confidence – not lack of technical knowledge or administrative incompetence – is, without exception, a prime factor with failing salesmen.

How can we improve our Self-confidence?

As I said before, self-confidence must not be confused with arrogance or brashness: to have a positive impact, self-confidence must be aligned with reality. For this reason, our old buddy self-awareness is an essential pre-requisite for realistic self-confidence.

We all have an 'inner map' of our own skills, abilities and weaknesses. Often, though, our perception of ourself is not accurate and we are actually far more able than we think we are.

I am sure you will have heard of or read Norman Vincent Peale's *'The power of positive thinking'*; some people think the book is wonderful, others don't get past the first chapter, believing that the author is asking them to do 'mental conjuring tricks' and pretending to be someone they are not.

Think of situations and areas of your life where you know you are confident and in control. You are essentially the same person in the sales environment, where you may not feel so confident. Make the connection between the two and realise that your innate ability is the same, in any area of your life.

For example, one young man who viewed himself as skilled at personal public relations, able to carry off a sales call or interview with confidence and style, felt shy in his personal life, whether at a party or on a date. Once he realised he was the same person in both situations, his self-confidence soared.

We must stop compartmentalising, putting different areas of our lives into separate boxes; then we will start making the essential connections that should enable us to be far more self-confident in the sales arena.

Nelson Mandela

Don't expect too much too soon: Rome wasn't built in a day. However, by systematic efforts to be more assertive over time, we can grow in self-confidence. Finally, if you are still struggling with low self-esteem, reflect on the words of Nelson Mandela in his inaugural presidential speech:

"We ask ourselves: Who am I to be brilliant, gorgeous, talented, fabulous?" Actually, who are you not to be? You are a child of God.

Your playing small doesn't serve the world. There is nothing enlightening about shrinking so that other people around you won't feel insecure. We are all meant to shine as children do.

We are born to manifest the glory of God that is within us. It is not just in some of us: it is in everyone. And as we let our light shine, we unconsciously give other people permission to do the same. As we are liberated from our own fear, our presence automatically releases others."

Chapter Eleven

MANAGING OURSELVES

Managing ourselves is all about ordering our 'inner life': managing and controlling our impulses, emotions and internal states. Like self-awareness, it is crucial in successful selling.

Now, more than ever, we are operating in a climate of fear, coupled with difficult economic conditions, especially in the service sector. To overcome this, we need strong inner resources, not more wretched techniques which only affect the 'outside' of the salesman.

In the fast-paced, edgy western world, where nothing is simple, a calm inner life is crucial to sales success. Successful selling is impossible when our emotions are unstable; physical changes take place within the brain that render us incapable of rational thought and we 'switch off'.

Let me illustrate with an anecdote told by Daniel Goleman from 'Working with Emotional Intelligence'. His friend, a psychologist, had flown to Hawaii to address a Convention of police chiefs. Exhausted and jet-lagged, he began by telling a joke, only to freeze, his mind a blank – he forgot the punch-line. Not only couldn't he remember the punch line, he couldn't remember his speech. He apologised and left the podium. After several hours' rest he returned to give his lecture – including the complete joke – to great applause.

Managing our emotions

The single most striking finding from brain studies of people under stress shows the emotional brain at work, undermining the workings of the brain's executive centre, the pre-frontal lobes, located just behind the forehead. In layman's terms, when an individual is under stress, the brain shifts into a 'self-protective', survival mode, stealing resources from 'working memory' and shunting them to other brain sites in order to keep the senses hyper-alert: a mental stance geared for survival.

The brain falls back on simple, familiar routines and blanks out complex thought, rational analysis and long-term planning. Self- protection at it's most basic. For Goleman's friend, this emergency mode, caused by stress, paralysed his ability to 'access' his speech, which was buried deep down in his executive memory.

Whilst the mental 'circuitry' for dealing with stress evolved millions of years ago, we experience its operation today in the form of troubling emotions: anxiety, fear, frustration, anger and irritation.

When studying salespeople who are failing, it is almost inevitable that this same process can be observed. Their emotions are paralysing their ability to act and find a way out of their difficulties. It may be that factors outside their sales career are producing these negative emotions: ill health, marriage breakdown, money worries, all made worse by the angst-ridden pace of life post 9/11.

If you can identify with this, there is some good news. Life's difficulties are often thrown at us in order that we 'dig deeper' and are toughened up by the circumstances we face. It is not the circumstances in themselves that cause the stress, but how we react to them. Read that sentence again s l o w l y, because it is so important.

Ah, but Laurie, it's easy for you to say that, but you just don't know what I am facing. From my personal experience, I had to cope with the suicide of both my father and uncle, the latter in especially gory circumstances, and I lived to tell the tale. I'm not for one minute claiming to be superman, but it was how I reacted that was important.

As Billy Connolly memorably said *"there is no such thing as the wrong weather – only the wrong clothes"*. Think about it.

If you are going through difficult times which are affecting your sales performance, use all the emotional resources you can to combat negative emotions. Don't be ashamed to ask others for support.

Read a biography of someone like the missionary Dr David Livingstone, who achieved incredible things against the odds – including the small matter of the abolition of the slave trade – by responding to stress in a positive way. 'When the going gets tough, the tough get going' is a hackneyed cliché, but it's true.

Take action

Get going. Refuse to let your circumstances – and the negative emotions they produce – control your sales career. Be real. Admit the difficulties. Be honest with yourself, then you're at least half the way there.

Again, getting up close and personal, I have found my Christian faith an incredible strength in my sales career – especially in the tough times. Prayer works.

We all need a 'centre of calm' from which to operate, whether it be a happy marriage, spiritual faith, fulfilling family life, good friends. It is difficult to maintain equilibrium with –out these.

I am by nature quite emotional, and left to my own devices would find it easy to succumb to anxiety and depression. However, on a purely pragmatic, hard-headed level, my faith has helped me to remain calm and focussed, able to retain control over my sales career, rather than allowing negative emotions to paralyse my actions.

The notion of emotional self-control does not mean denying or repressing true feelings, but *recognising* them. 'Bad' moods can have their uses: anger, sadness and fear can become sources of creativity and energy. Anger, when managed properly, rather than corroding a situation like leaked battery acid, can be an intense source of motivation. The urgency born of anxiety – as long as it is not overwhelming – can be the catalyst for creativity and change.

Artists and actors use both negative and positive emotions creatively, to produce great performances. As mentioned earlier, it is not the circumstances but our emotional response to those circumstances that dictate success or failure. Remember Billy Connolly: *"there is no such thing as the wrong weather, only the wrong clothes."*

Chapter Twelve

OVERCOMING FEAR

Fear is a powerful emotion. We must recognise that, as salespeople, we are not immune to the fear and negativity that permeates western culture post 9/11. We read the same newspapers, watch the same television programmes as our customers; we are bombarded with negative images, child murder, bad news, horror and war.

We know that the majority of buying decisions are based on emotion, rather than reason. There are exceptions – I imagine that rocket scientists might veer more towards reason – but if you are to be successful in this tough arena, a client's fear must be faced head on, not ignored.

The key issue is, though – how can you deal with the fear in another person if you have not mastered your own fears? As always, the first step is to be honest with yourself and acknowledge your own fear. You may never have thought about this before. You may never have had time to sit quietly and wonder why all those 'Close that Sale' textbooks you bought at a sales convention have not worked for you.

Overcoming fear may be a turning point in significantly increasing our earnings, turning failure into success.

The media fuels this 'black rain' of fear – remember, bad news sells newspapers. For a superb analysis of the subject, read Tom Davies' *'Merlin the Magician and the Pacific Coast Highway'*, published by New English Library.

Fear is one of the most corrosive and infectious of emotions and we can 'catch' it from our clients and the media. So, having acknowledged it, what can we do about it?

Stop fuelling your fear

Selling into the current environment is difficult, because we can easily become infected with the same fears that our clients struggle with. We know that what we put into our body (ie. eat) determines our physical health; in the same way, what we feed ourselves on mentally will determine our mental health.

This is not about mental conjuring tricks. Although I am not a great fan of self- hypnosis, I do understand that it probably works because, if you feed yourself the same message often enough, you begin to believe it.

Totalitarian regimes thrive on propaganda and Adolf Hitler understood how important this was by appointing Dr Josef Goebbels as his Minister of Information (ie. propaganda). It's interesting how close the words minister and sinister are.

Again, it's back to our old friend truth. Instead of feeding yourself on fear and lies, make a deliberate decision to reverse the process by feeding yourself with positives. You have to do it, nobody else can do it for you.

It may mean radically changing your reading, viewing and listening habits, making a conscious decision to 'accentuate the positive and eliminate the negative', as the old song goes.

It surprises me that some salespeople have no awareness of this and watch horror movies by the dozen, feeding themselves voraciously on tabloid headlines celebrating war, sleaze and dishonesty... and then do their first sales call, expecting to be positive and focussed!

Stop feeding the vulture (and culture) of negativity. Watch movies that are life-affirming. Kick out Lethal Indecent Proposed Nightmare ('The Final Awakening before last') and watch Notting Hill.

"Darling... is that Ground Force starting...?"

Stop reading the tabloid financial pages which only fuel your depression and embeds bad news into your psyche, helping you to find more reasons to fail: instead, read an article in a Sunday paper about Future Hope, a charity in Calcutta where life is being affirmed, children given a real hope rather than a lingering death.

Nothing wrong with 'airport' novels. John Grisham is a good writer. But why not, on your next long journey, read Paulo Coelho's 'The Alchemist' (HarperCollins £6.99, paperback), a magical fable which affirms life's potential, rather than life's disasters. Read Alexander McCall Smith's 'The No. 1 Ladies Detective Agency' (Polygon) to discover a good, positive side to Africa (*'lots of people living decent lives in difficult circumstances'*, to quote the author) and have a good laugh into the bargain.

Avoid Saloon Bar Doom Merchants

Be careful who you spend time with. We are known by the company we keep; just make sure that you are spending time with colleagues and friends who are positive and uplifting company, rather than the doom merchants you can spot in any saloon bar in the country. Negative people will drag you down, especially those with a penchant for large quantities of the hard stuff.

Enthusiasm and a positive mental attitude are infectious, so make sure you surround yourself with upbeat characters who will bring out the best in you. After all, it is your livelihood that is at stake and you may have to take some pretty drastic steps to ensure your survival.

Chapter Thirteen

OVERCOMING ANGER

First cousin to fear is anger. In the modern sales environment, there are so many potential triggers for anger. Unrealistic sales targets, stifling regulation, tailbacks on motorways, genghis khan-like sales managers, constant staff changes, litigation culture, red tape, parking problems.... the list is endless.

If we fail to manage our anger effectively, we can end up as a heart attack waiting to happen or, at the very least, this most damaging of emotions will paralyse our effective sales performance. How the Reverend Ian Paisley has avoided a coronary is beyond me. That man is angry. How anyone can call him Reverend is also beyond me.

Six friends, all in University, were drinking and playing cards late into the night. An argument broke out. Ray and Tom's disagreement became louder and angrier until Ray flew into a rage, screaming and shouting; at this point Tom became noticeably calm and cool.

Ray's temper was now out of control and his anger was his master: he challenged Tom to a fight. Tom responded calmly, stating that he would consider a punch-up, but only once they had finished the card game. Ray, although red with rage, agreed. During the time it took to conclude the game, Ray settled down and collected his thoughts and no fight ensued.

Fast forward the tape twenty years later to a University reunion. Tom, the calm and collected one, was a highly successful executive in the music business, whilst Ray... was out of work, struggling with alcohol and drug addiction. The stark contrast between the two is ample testimony to the immense benefits of being able to say no to anger. *It is a choice.*

Marshmallow kids

The story neatly parallels that of two groups of children who were part of an experiment called the 'marshmallow test', undertaken at Stanford University in the US. Four year-olds in the local kindergarten were brought into a room one by one, a marshmallow was put on the table in front of them and they were told "you can eat this marshmallow now if you want, but if you don't eat it until after I run an errand, you can have two when I return."

Fourteen years later when graduating from High School, the children who ate the marshmallow straight away were compared with those who waited and received two. Those who grabbed, compared to those who waited, were more likely to fall apart under stress, became irritable and aggressive and were more likely to be dishonest in pursuit of their goals.

What the researchers found most surprising, though, was a completely unforeseen consequence: those children who had waited for the marshmallow had scores averaging a remarkable 210 points higher in their University entrance exam than those who grabbed the sweet first time. Research suggests a strong link between impulsivity and diminished learning ability.

If we are preoccupied by emotionally driven thoughts, there is that much less 'space' in our rational brain to make positive, rational decisions.

What has this got to do with selling? A great deal. The story of the marshmallow kids teaches us profound lessons about the cost of emotions that are out of control. When in the grip of anger, fear and impulse, our ability to think – and our sales success – will suffer.

Now I'm not saying that overcoming anger is easy (I still struggle) but if we can learn to manage this most crippling of emotions, we will set ourselves free to achieve sales performance we have only dreamt of. I am not, however, talking about over-control and the stifling of feelings and spontaneity. In fact, there is a physical and mental cost to such over-control. People who stifle their emotions, especially strong negative ones, raise their heart rate, a sure sign of increased tension.

Some cultures, especially those in Asia, encourage this pattern of masking negative feelings. Whilst this may keep relationships tranquil, it will come at a cost to the repressed individual. A psychologist teaching emotional intelligence competence to flight attendants on Asian airlines said "imploding is the problem there. They don't explode, but hold it in and suffer." This repression of feelings may not manifest itself outwardly, but the internal damage may express itself in headaches, smoking and drinking too much, edginess, self-criticism and sleeplessness.

We need to find appropriate ways to manage our emotions, rather than stifle them altogether. We may feel anger and rage well up inside us, but we need to distance ourself from the emotion and express how we are feeling, but without anger.

Can I suggest that a good way to start is to learn to handle anger in others, because learning this skill will assist us enormously in managing ourself. Look at the following case study...

Bill Gates – Charmless Nerd

Fred Moody in 'Wonder women in the Rude Boys' Paradise', Fast Company, June/July 1996, tells the story of a Bill Gates outburst and one woman's skill at handling it.

'Bill Gates is pissed. His eyes are bulging and his oversized glasses are askew. His face is flushed and spit is flying from his mouth. He's in a small, crowded conference room at the Microsoft campus with 20 young Microsofties gathered around an oblong table. Most look at their chairman with outright fear, if they look at him at all. The sour smell of sweaty terror fills the room.

While Gates continues his angry tirade, the hapless programmers fumble and stutter, trying to placate him. Nobody seems to be able to get through – except a small, soft-spoken Chinese-American woman, seemingly the only person in the room who is unfazed by his tantrums. She looks him in the eye while everyone else avoids eye contact.

Twice she interrupts his tirade to address him in quiet tones. The first time, her words seem to calm him a little, before his shouting resumes. The second time, he listens in silence, thoughtfully gazing down at the table. Suddenly, his anger evaporates and he tells her, "Okay, this looks good. Go ahead." With that, he ends the meeting'.

The direct eye contact sent Gates a subliminal message that she was not afraid of him. What the woman said was little different from what her colleagues had been saying. But her unflappability, and refusal to allow herself to be infected by (a) her colleagues' anxiety and (b) Bill Gates' anger, were huge factors in allowing her to say clearly what needed to be said. There is a proverb which says 'A gentle answer turns away wrath'. How true.

Take control of your emotions

So often, we allow ourselves to suffer because of other people's out of control emotions. Why? Maybe because we think that in some way we are to blame; perhaps a lack of self-esteem.

We sometimes sign for guilt that is not ours. We need to learn to detach ourself from others' emotions and then will be able to learn to manage our own.

We need to take control of our own state of mind. Moods exert a powerful pull on thought, perception and memory. When we are angry, our thoughts become pre-occupied with the object of our anger and our irritability completely distorts our perspective. Perfectly benign comments can strike us as hostile, if we are enveloped by the red rain of anger.

You can't sell effectively if your emotions are controlling you, rather than the other way around. Managing anger is an absolute key to being freed to think straight. Don't rationalise your anger – deal with it.

Music has a particularly soothing effect. If you are feeling really wound up, put on a suitable CD (perhaps not The Clash's Greatest Hits), music that will calm your mood. Who knows, you may even find yourself buying a Mozart sampler.

Chapter Fourteen

INTEGRITY

When times are hard, it is very tempting to cut corners. Ken Lloyd, Ph.D, in his *'Keep it simple Guide to Selling'* (Dorling Kindersley £12.99) says *"Some people naively ask if it is possible to be an ethical salesperson and a successful salesperson at the same time. The implication is that to do well in sales, you have to be a little skilful in deceit. Nothing could be further from the truth. If you want to be a truly successful salesperson, you have to be ethical."*

I agree wholeheartedly. A few of my clients have said "I couldn't do your job in a month of Sundays. Surely you need the gift of the gab and anyway, I couldn't persuade people to buy what they didn't want."

Embedded deep in the British psyche is an innate distrust of salespeople, based on the stereotype hard-living, fast-driving, flash operator, who will state categorically that his mother is the Queen of Sheba in order to get a sale.

Del Boy

Del Trotter from *'Only Fools and Horses'* is a national treasure, regularly coming top in UK Viewers' polls, for two reasons: David Jason is an exceptional actor and Del Boy is such an easily recognisable stereotype. In fact, if I were running a training course majoring on integrity, I could do little better than show an episode of the Series and just tell the delegates to do precisely the opposite!

Selling is still seen by many as an aggressive act you **do** to the customer. This attitude is perhaps especially prevalent amongst the retired and elderly, many of whom watch Only Fools & Horses. We have to be aware that this is how we may be perceived, so we need to bend over backwards to correct this impression.

My wife Brenda used to work for a firm of South Coast Estate Agents in the late seventies. She said that telling lies was so ingrained that even when telling the truth would have been to the negotiators' advantage, they still told untruths out of habit! Please don't take it personally if you are an estate agent, because I know many of you to be honest, conscientious and reliable.

One of the best pieces of advice I was ever given was when I first came into selling in the early 80s. A work colleague of mine said "Imagine you are the Client. If you wouldn't take your own advice, then something is wrong."

Elsewhere in the book I talk about how important it is to build long-term relationships with clients; this can only be done with integrity and honesty as the cornerstones.

Ken Lloyd: *"When salespeople stray from the truth, it is not long before their customers stray from them."* Ethical salespeople really care about their clients, having a real sense of respect and concern for them. I talk elsewhere about mimicry and pretence in selling, resulting in shallow, pseudo-relationships with customers.

Trying to talk a prospect into buying a product or service that does not meet his/her needs shows a lack of integrity. We may find it difficult, but given that situation the right thing to do is to say "sorry, but I don't think we have the right product for you. I wish I could help, but I would be doing you a dis-service by trying to sell you this."

My close friend Mike Jones, M.D. of his own Accountancy Practice, has been an inspiration to me in this regard. Integrity is his watchword and it permeates all his business dealings, resulting in a large and loyal client base.

Honesty makes good commercial sense – as well as being the right thing to do – because word gets around and one soon acquires a reputation for ethics and probity. Remember it takes 25 years to build a reputation and 5 minutes to destroy it, although it doesn't seem to bother Jeffrey Archer.

No Income Tax, no VAT

I have one or two clients who take great delight in telling me that they pay far less tax than they should. The plumber who earns £35,000 p.a. but records £12,000; the car mechanic who always insist that you pay cash. 'No income tax, no VAT', as the Only Fools & Horses theme tune goes. They think they are being so clever but they are unconsciously telling me so much about themselves. If they are diddling the tax-man, it is probable that they are also stitching me up!

I am often tempted to make that anonymous telephone call to the Inland Revenue and rat on them, because the taxes I pay are in effect subsidising this black economy. We get all self-righteous when we see Robert Mugabe, Zimbabwe's power-crazy dictator robbing white farmers of their homes, so why don't we apply the same logic to our countrymen? Ok, they are not murdering and pillaging, but the principle is the same.

Ah, but everybody does it. Do they? Someone who is dishonest in small things is likely, given the opportunity, to be dishonest in big things; but someone who is honest in the little things, is likely to have the same integrity when dealing with larger transactions.

Loveable rogues?

We need to stop admiring people like Ronnie Biggs who appear to have 'got away with it'. He hasn't. If you have seen recent photos of him you'll see what I mean. Years of so called easy living and excess, fuelled by the 'fruits' of his dishonesty, have caught up with him. The very cash that he embezzled has led to his downfall.

I don't generally buy into the notion of the loveable rogue. I haven't come across too many of them. Rogue... yes. Loveable... generally not, as any of the petrified tenants of Nicholas van Hoogstraten, murderous Brighton property tycoon – now serving a life sentence – will readily testify. Perhaps Robin Hood was an exception, since we are led to believe that he at least re-distributed wealth to the poor.

In addition to maintaining integrity in our dealings with clients, it is equally important to practice the same standards in relation to our Company. It never ceases to amaze me how many salesmen leave their job and move to a rival organisation, totally ignoring the contract they originally signed forbidding them from contacting their ex-Company's clients.

These people have burned their bridges, will get a poor reference and an even worse reputation. Most salespersons subscribe (at least in theory) to a Company's code of ethics in relation to customers, but integrity often goes out of the window when they are dealing with their Employer.

Dr Ken Lloyd again: *"When salespeople engage in unethical actions, it is a matter of time before their exploits are discovered. Customers (and indeed employers) do not regard lies, deceit, mis-representations, over-statements and other types of self-serving behaviour too fondly. When they discover that a salesperson has acted unethically, it spells the end of the sale, the end of future business, the end of referrals, and the end of the salesperson's good name."* Not worth it, is it?

Dishonesty always catches up with you, sooner or later. Remember, the great thing about telling the truth is that you don't have to remember what you said.

You reap what you sow.

Reliability

Reliability and integrity are closely related. Ken Lloyd again: *"Ethical salespeople are reliable and keep their commitments. If you come back to a customer with excuses and changes as to why some of your commitments haven't been met, you undermine not only the sale, but your relationship with the customer as well."*

This again is especially crucial when times are difficult. Let's start with punctuality. As a kid, I was dreadful at this, probably as an over-reaction against a civil servant father who obsessively arrived everywhere 2 hours early, with me reluctantly in tow. I remember waiting aimlessly on railway stations, the wind whistling down the platform from a brisk, north-easterly direction, vowing that when I grew up I wouldn't be the same.

I probably over-reacted a bit and as a teenager was hopelessly late for everything. Being both a sportsman and a musician, I once arrived at a booking to play bass guitar at around 8.30p.m. The event had started at 7.30 and my band were well into the sixth song in the set. The only problem was... I was still in full cricket gear, whites and all, because I hadn't allowed enough time to get to the venue.

Punctuality is not an out-dated virtue because it is almost always a clue to our reliability – or the opposite. It is especially valued amongst older customers, being seen as an essential virtue in a professional of any description. It is the first thing that a potential customer will notice about us; remember that prospective purchasers are forming judgements about us in the first 10 to 15 minutes, subconsciously making up their minds as to whether they can enter into a business relationship with us.

Being late is also rude. Or at least, in western culture, that is how it is interpreted. It is a different matter in cultures such as Africa and the sub-continent, where the concept of time can be very different! In the West, turning up late sends out the message that your previous appointment was more important, in the same way that the salesperson who takes a telephone call on his mobile during a meeting, subconsciously communicates that his phone conversation is more important than his current customer. Had you thought about that?

There are circumstances where you can't avoid being late. Now is the time to use your mobile and call your client, apologising that you will be late. I sometimes have representatives of Insurance Companies wandering in at 1.15pm for a 12.30 appointment, no apology, and they wonder why I'm not all that interested in their products. Have the words "I'm sorry" disappeared from the English language? Don't take your customers for granted.

If you can recognise yourself here, *change your behaviour*. This doesn't require years in therapy, just thinking logically and planning your day effectively, building a little 'slack' into your timetable, not starting on a long telephone call just prior to setting out for an appointment.

Be Conscientious

There are many studies which link superior sales performance to this quality. Barrick, Mount & Strauss, in their study *'Conscientiousness and Performance of Sales Representatives'*, found that outstanding effectiveness depended on conscientiousness.

In the current economic climate, it has been found that this quality is highly valued amongst Employers, almost as much as the volume of sales made. Another 'old-fashioned' virtue maybe, but when times are tough we need to dig deep and strengthen ourselves on the inside, using the difficulties we face to develop our 'inner man'.

It was Albert Einstein (and he knew a thing or two) who said *"In the middle of every difficulty lies opportunity."*

Work harder

When conditions are tough we need to work harder. Talking of working harder, let me tell you about a young lad called Victor. I encountered him on a recent trip to Uganda, where I had gone with a church team to assist and encourage small business projects in and around Kampala, the capital.

He spent 12 hours in the hot African sun, selling secondhand clothes with the aid of a rusty bike, cycling about 25 miles. His net return for the day? 100 Ugandan shillings – the equivalent of 12 pence. It is the very adversity of his circumstances which is the motivating force for his hard work and con- scientiousness and we can learn a lot from him.

In the midst of difficulty, finding opportunity.

Adaptability and Innovation

You may remember a TV programme in the early 90s called Troubleshooter, presented by the former Chairman of Shell, Sir John Harvey-Jones. His brief was to visit Companies of varying sizes who were struggling, and give their directors the benefit of his years of experience and expertise in running a very successful public Company.

He visited the classic car manufacturer Morgan, and what followed illustrated how businesses stagnate when change is resisted and there is little willingness to adapt. Sir John had the temerity to suggest that they should increase their annual production of cars by a very small percentage, which encountered fierce resistance and a supercilious attitude from the Morgan directors.

There was a five year waiting list for new cars, and rather than this being a source of deep concern, the Morgan journeymen saw this as enhancing the prestige of the marque. The fact that hundreds on the waiting list would get fed up waiting and transfer their allegiance to another prestige manufacturer, with a 3 month delivery time, had never permeated their smug, inflexible thought processes.

God forbid that we should be the same, but we need to examine our attitudes, especially when business is scarce and we are not sure where the next sale is coming from. Difficult times often demand drastic measures. Necessity is indeed the mother of invention and we need to be open to look hard and long at our current business mix and see whether we need to innovate and change; perhaps, as it were, we need to 'fish in a different pool'.

In the business I know best, financial services, because of the long bear run on the stockmarket, clients are very reluctant to invest lump sums; one almost has to surgically remove a client's cheque book. There is a great wall of money currently sitting on deposit.

We need to recognise that circumstances have drastically changed since the late 90s and find new markets – or revisit

"No..! No... not my cheque book! Take my arm instead..."

old ones – and fresh ideas: equity release schemes, life assurance, inheritance tax planning, property funds, to name but a few.

Adaptability is so important when it comes to handling our clients. Business can be lost because we insist on following our agenda, rather than being adaptable and allowing the Client to set the agenda. Insecurity may lead you to over-control the proceedings and the client will feel stifled, not allowed to express what is important to her.

The best salesmen are the most adaptable: secure in their own abilities, they are happy for the client to take the lead, knowing that their sales skills will enable them to cover all the points they want to cover. Not what many sales text-books will tell you!

The innovator takes real pleasure in innovation: it gives him a 'buzz'. People who have this knack quickly identify key issues and simplify problems that seem overwhelmingly complex. Those without this skill, by contrast, typically miss the wider picture and get bogged down in detail, and therefore deal with complex problems slowly and laboriously.

Chapter Fifteen

MOTIVATION

The Institute of Manpower Studies says that the word 'motivation' is among the six most used words in company documents. It goes on to say that just because the word is used, it doesn't mean to say that it is understood.

In a survey carried out by the Grassroots Group plc, which included 500 of the top 1000 businesses in the UK, it was found that 95% of those companies that responded felt that their staff could be more motivated.

The foundation of all motivation is hope. If you really don't believe that you can do something, then you probably won't. But I have found it true that 'if you have faith like a grain of mustard seed, you can move mountains', to quote the words of Jesus. In other words, just a small amount, maybe even 1%, belief that you can achieve a particular goal will get you there. Isn't that amazing?

A friend of mine in Financial Services had been going through a very bad time, allowing himself to be depressed by all the bad news around, to such an extent that he was becoming de-motivated and paralysed into inaction. He was due to sit an examination and was not looking forward to it. Rather to his surprise he passed and just by taking this small step of positive action, his whole attitude changed. When we lose hope, inertia takes over and we lose motivation.

I went through a very sticky patch many years ago. Few appointments in the diary, bills to pay and not much money coming in. In desperation, I telephoned my good friend Alan Hiscox for advice. Alan is a highly accomplished pianist and so I expected a reply similar to a grade 8 Chopin piano piece – creative and complex.

I was not really expecting his response: "just get out of the office and see people – it really doesn't matter whom, just take action." I was expecting something far more profound and thought this much too simplistic.

However, I swallowed hard, took the medicine and within hours of taking the advice, my whole attitude and demeanour changed, as if by magic.

Motivation is a vast subject and there is a whole library of books on the topic, together with a growing army of motivational speakers.

Here are four aspects of motivation which typify out-standing salesmen:

(1) **Achievement drive:** Striving to improve or meet a standard of excellence.

(2) **Mental Toughness:** Not falling apart when things are tough.

(3) **Goal-setting:** Setting realistic personal targets and having the self-discipline to achieve them.

(4) **Initiative & Optimism:** Seizing opportunities and taking obstacles and setbacks in one's stride.

What is Motivation?

We will look at these four aspects in more detail in a moment, but let us examine the subject in general terms first. As with a number of skills, the specific competence comes into sharp focus especially when it is absent. How many times have we described struggling fellow salesmen as lacking that 'certain something'? Usually that certain something is motivation.

In difficult times, it can be very tempting to resign ourselves to poor sales performance, because we can always point to circumstances and blame them for lack of success. Let's be real: I know that it is not always easy to stay focussed and positive when bombarded with bad news via the media, together with anxious telephone calls from clients who dump their anxieties and fears on us. It can be emotionally debilitating and, if left unchecked, will wear us down and undermine our motivation.

It may be worth taking a few minutes to reflect on what motivates us to do our sales job. Here are some suggestions, by no means exhaustive:

● **Money**

● **Status**

● **Contact with people**

● **Material possessions**

● **Helping people**

If we are going through a rough time, it can be helpful to remind ourself why we went into selling in the first place, because re-visiting these initial goals will have a strong motivating impact. If all those years ago, a major goal for you was retirement at 55 to a small Caribbean island, display a picture on your wall of that small Caribbean island, as a reminder of why you are still slogging away. It will help to keep you focussed.

You can continue to develop your positive expectations with the help of other photos that are somehow related to the attainment of these goals, such as pictures of you during successful events in your life. I know that sometimes in Sales it can get so bad that you really don't know where your next sale is coming from: if this is you, don't worry – you are not alone.

Instead, remind yourself of your abilities and past success by taking that photo of yourself at the Sales Convention receiving an award out of the cupboard, and putting it up on the wall. Keep feeding yourself positive messages.

The power of motivation

Richard Denny, described by the Daily Mail as the 'UK's guru of motivation' says in his book '*Motivate to Win*' – "*The power of motivation cannot be underestimated: it makes extraordinary achievements possible in every walk of life.*

Motivation is the inner power behind mankind's success and achievements. In maintaining or building your own motivation, search out stories of success. It depends very little on our age or colour, race or circumstances. YOU CAN IF YOU THINK YOU CAN."

Denny's book avoids the excesses of the 1970s motivational speakers, still traipsing around the speaking circuit in ill-fitting suits, being paid mega-bucks for re-cycling tired old cliches from 1970s Sales textbooks. *Avoid them at all costs*, because if you follow their dictums you will become a cartoon character. Thoughtful books like Denny's, however, I would commend to you since they contain real wisdom.

Denny mentions that significant achievement does not depend on circumstances. Indeed, if one looks at a wide variety of success stories, it seems that adverse circumstances are often a positive driving force. There is a nugget of gold here, which goes against all logical thought. There is a very real sense in which adversity is our friend, if we will but embrace it, rather than run away from it.

Adversity can be a friend

Nelson Mandela is a superb example of this. Incarcerated for 28 years by Voerwoerd's apartheid regime in South Africa, I'm sure we'll never forget those first pictures of him with wife Winnie, emerging into the sunshine surrounded by cheering crowds and the world's press. If anyone had good reason to be bitter and resentful, it was him. However, by forgiving his captors he chose to turn adversity into success and he would not be the much revered international statesman he is today, without those lonely years in jail on Robben Island.

Let us now move on to examine those aspects of motivation mentioned above, in more detail:

Achievement drive

I have never met a truly successful salesperson without this key quality. Michael Klepper and Robert Gunther (1997) in their study of the 100 wealthiest Americans throughout history – including Bill Gates and John D. Rockefeller – show that what they all share is their competitive drive: a single-minded passion for their business. High achievers are results-driven with a burning need to meet their goals and standards.

There is still quite a difference in attitudes to success between the UK and the US. The British still seem to have an inbuilt suspicion of success, almost automatically assuming that to become successful, the individual will have lied, bullied and cajoled his way to the top. Status, rather than business success, is probably still valued more this side of the pond. 'Old' money is perceived as somehow nobler, less tainted than 'new' money.

In the Land of Opportunity, however, success is valued and prized far more highly and Americans are less cynical about those who have achieved it. In this positive, affirming culture, is it any surprise that so many successful entrepreneurs have been grown in Stateside soil?

There is nothing inherently evil or 'grubby' about success per se: it's what you do with your money and how you are as a person that are important. Ah, but the old proverb says 'money is the root of all evil, surely?! No, this is often misquoted. The actual text says it is the *love* of money that is the root of all evil. That is something completely different.

W. Somerset Maugham wisely said:

"The common idea that success spoils people by making them vain, egotistical and self complacent is erroneous.

On the contrary, it makes them for the most part humble, tolerant and kind. Failure makes people cruel and bitter."

We need people to be successful, especially in selling, because it is no use producing a superb product if it sits on the shelf, gathering dust. It has to be sold for any profit to be made.

Selling in the Seventies and Eighties was relatively easy – at least easier than it is in the early 21st century. Times have changed and success in sales now demands much more, especially in terms of the inside of the salesman.

As businesses become leaner and fitter, so mentally we need to be the same, hence my emphasis on inner, personal qualities. I have said before that we should resist the temptation to compartmentalise our lives, instead seeing that the key topic of motivation is the same, whether we are salesmen or professional sportsmen.

Peter Lewis, CEO of US auto insurance company Progressive Insurance, is blunt about his drive for success. *"We demand a very high standard from our salespeople, but the rewards can be great – people can double their salary in bonuses. One of our core values is doing better than we did before. We strive constantly to meet and exceed the highest expectations of our customers, shareholders and people."*

Despite these high standards, the Company has a staff turnover rate of around 8%, the industry average, because those who gravitate towards the company share Lewis' commitment to high achievement.

Spencer & Spencer in their study Competence at Work, analysed 286 organisations in 21 countries. They found that achievement drive featured as the single most frequent distinguishing quality amongst superior executives.

Mental toughness

If you have any interest in sport, particularly team games such as cricket, rugby and football, you will already be convinced that it is the mental side of the game which distinguishes the good from the great. Outstanding performers such as Tiger Woods in golf or Sachin Tendulkar in cricket possess the same mental toughness and achievement drive which sets them apart from the rest of the pack.

There is so much we can learn by studying these top sportspeople. Are these qualities innate, or learnt? Whilst I am sure that a top performer needs to have a certain natural competitiveness, it is my belief that you and I can greatly improve our achievement drive and mental toughness. How? By constantly learning, **being teachable** and refusing to give up, even in trying circumstances. This will produce patience and tenacity, very helpful companions when the going is rough.

The absence of these qualities also has much to teach us. How much greater a tennis player would John McEnroe have been had he been tougher mentally, instead of allowing his emotions to hi-jack his playing ability? Perhaps it is no accident that his arch-rival Bjorn Borg, innately less talented, beat him so many times because of his single-minded achievement drive, manifesting itself in far superior mental toughness. Often McEnroe was playing not only his opponent, but his emotions and the whole Establishment as well.

Chapter Sixteen

GOAL SETTING

'If you fail to plan, you plan to fail' may be a cliché, but as with most clichés, contains truth. Very few people actually decide what it is they want and salesmen are no different. How do you know if you've hit the target, if you don't know what the target is?

Basic common sense, I hear you murmuring. However, it is really surprising when you ask people what they want that so few can actually tell you. One tends to hear vague answers such as "I want to be a millionaire" or "I want to be happy". Upon being asked how they are going to achieve this, I am often told "we'll continue as we are for a few years and then review the situation, something will turn up."

More than ever in tough times, sales success depends on setting realistic, achievable goals and then exercising the self-discipline to make it happen. Self-discipline is persistence by another name.

Here are some key questions and points to bear in mind when setting goals:

What do you really want?

List your deepest desires, both short and long term, in your business and personal life. Be realistic. Avoid jotting down things just because you feel you ought to. Don't just put down financial goals because, although short-term they can be motivational (eg. getting out of debt!), money is often the means to the goal, rather than the goal itself.

Remember my earlier example of the desire to retire at age 55 to a Caribbean island. That is the goal, rather than money – the latter is simply the means by which to achieve it.

What is your precise goal?

Select from your list a primary goal, taking into account (a) that it should be worth the effort, (b) it should be possible in months, not years and (c) it is achievable.

Richard Denny says *"I have heard motivational trainers say to their audiences 'set big goals'. They are wrong. And it can be dangerous. It may sound highly motivational in a convention hall, but the danger is that short-term goals which are too big don't become believable and are not achieved. The goal setter becomes demotivated and, in some cases, never tries again. Big goals can be set long term."*

I agree wholeheartedly. Don't be too tough with yourself, especially if you are already feeling low; set goals that you can genuinely believe for and the very act of setting the goal and meaning it, will make you feel better. It will also give you a real sense that you are in control of your destiny, rather than at the whim of circumstance.

Your target should be both measurable and quantifiable; If your short term goal is buying a new car, what make and model? What colour and which extras? This will help immensely with the next point.

Visualise fulfilment of the goal

This will help you immensely with self-motivation. Visualise the achievement of the goal, with the attendant feelings of warmth and anticipation. We do this all the time without even consciously being aware of it.

Imagine you are looking forward to a well-planned holiday: you will start to day-dream, or visualise yourself by the pool, with a good book and a Baileys on ice. You can almost feel the sunshine on your face and the feelings of pleasure and contentment.

Let your brain play an active part in helping you towards your goal. Roger Bannister, the first man in the world to run a mile in under four minutes, visualised running four separate quarter miles, and each quarter mile was achieved in under a minute. That is how to precisely define your goal and turn dreams into reality.

Set a realistic deadline

The deadline should not be too far away, otherwise like homework when we were at school, we will leave it to the last minute. As a writer, I need to put myself under a certain degree of pressure in order to achieve the goal, ie. the finishing of the book. We all respond to deadlines: every year, Christmas shopping is done by the vast majority in the last two weeks, despite resolutions to do their shopping earlier than last year. Simple but true: Deadlines are a great motivator.

Reward yourself along the way

It can be lonely in selling because once all the turbo-charged bonhomie, exchange of business cards and backslapping of the annual sales Convention is over, it's just you and the diary.

If your goal is making 8 new sales appointments over the next 3 days, break the goals down into even smaller chunks and reward yourself as you achieve each chunk.

Once you've achieved, say 3, instead of sandwiches in the office, take a friend out to Pizza Express. If he asks why, tell him and this will reinforce your self-confidence and feeling of achievement.

When I'm writing, I will set myself a number of small goals during a writing day, and when I achieve them I give myself a little reward, eg. once I have written say 300 words, I get a cup of tea. Not quantum physics, admittedly, but it works for me. Remember the one 70s sales nostrum that is worth repeating, although a little tired.... 'By the yard, it's hard; by the inch, it's a cinch'.

This book is called Sales Success in Tough Times. These are Tough Times and if you can succeed now, you can succeed in any conditions that come along. Be kind to yourself – it will also help with feelings of self-worth because our self-esteem usually takes a battering when things are rough.

Carry a Reminder

Surely that's going too far – a bit self-conscious, isn't it? No. Carry a written statement of your goals in handbag or wallet as a reminder, not only of the actual goals, but that you are taking control of your destiny. By carrying your goals, if you experience setbacks – which you surely will – or someone else tries to sidetrack you from achieving them, there they are, written down in a diary or on a card, as a constant reminder.

I don't know about you, but I don't mind looking silly if I end up a multi-millionaire!

Make a written plan

Take a sheet of paper, write the exact goal on the top plus the
date by which it is to be achieved. Then make a list of all the
stages necessary along the way to achieving the goal. Each
stage of the plan should have its own dated deadline.

Why is it difficult?

If it is just common sense, why doesn't everyone get what they
want in life? It may be that they don't really want it enough
and so are not prepared to put in the extra effort needed. More
commonly, though, people will look for reasons why they
can't achieve the goal. Why? Deep down, they don't believe
they can do it or have had so much negative 'programming'
in childhood that their self-confidence has been shattered.

Remember though that a tiny bit of faith can move
mountains: start with the miniscule amount of belief that you
have and you will be surprised at the results.

Keep the right company. When we are struggling, it is very
important that we surround ourself with others who are
positive, who will do us good rather than drag us down.

Avoid those who will give you lots of good reasons as to why
it is understandable that you are failing (they probably are as
well). Avoid like the plague those who talk about themselves
incessantly, droning on about all their woes and who drain
your emotional energy, giving back nothing in return.

Why is Self-discipline important?

In earlier chapters I have talked about managing ourselves
and it almost goes without saying that self-discipline is crucial
to the success of your goal-setting. So many good intentions
– including goal-setting – come to nothing if we lack the self-
discipline to persevere.

Three years ago I set myself a goal: to learn to play the piano up to grade 5 standard. I broke down the goal into a number of steps, but realised that self-discipline in this area had not always been my strongest suit.

When I was 13 (I am now 55) I tried to learn piano, but would never practise and so my piano teacher told my parents after 3 months that my further attendance "was a waste of their money". What an honest salesperson she was.

However, I now find that the self-discipline imposed on me by the four half hour practice sessions between weekly lessons is the means of achieving my goal. Like Gromit in the hilarious film The Wrong Trousers, build yourself a track to run on.

Look for ways of imposing discipline and structure on yourself; it is almost inevitable that you will have to drop something in order to release the time needed to enable you to achieve your goal. Look at your diary and ask yourself whether everything you do is strictly necessary. If you want your goal badly enough, you will find the time.

Chapter Seventeen

INITIATIVE AND OPTIMISM

I am sure you have heard the expressions 'seize the day' and 'faint heart never won fair lady'. Because these expressions are so familiar, we often ignore the pearls of wisdom they contain. If you look back to major successes you have had in life, you will see that most of these needed real initiative, perhaps even a touch of daring. When you proposed to your wife, or moved to a different part of the country, it took both initiative and optimism.

Is the glass half-empty or half-full? In tough times, with the fabric of society fragmenting, it is easy to see the glass as half empty and allow this to paralyse the taking of initiative. Don't think for one minute that the Gurus of Motivation mentioned earlier don't have periods of self-doubt.

I am sure Anthony Robbins has the odd rough patch, but of course his public persona may not allow him to show it. Personally, I prefer my heroes 'warts and all' and often learn most from those who are prepared to be vulnerable and admit to bouts of gloom and pessimism.

Sales success doesn't just happen. You have to initiate. People with initiative act before they are forced to do so by external events. J.Michael Crant, in his study of initiative within the estate agency profession, noted that estate agents could simply wait for the phone to ring, or they could study classified ads for houses being sold by owners and approach them to register with their firm. Unsurprisingly, the study found that the greater initiative shown resulted in more houses sold and higher commission earnings.

Initiative often requires a combination of enterprise and daring, taking the risk that either we will be rejected or look silly. Take the case of the shipping clerk in the US who worked out that his Company did sufficient business with Federal Express to qualify not only for a discount, but a dedicated computer to progress-chase orders. The clerk boldly suggested the idea to the C.E.O., it was accepted and saved the Company $30,000.

These days, we may be more familiar with the term proactive, but this is essentially the same as taking initiative. As a professional salesperson, you should be proactive, not reactive, in your relationships with your customers. So often I have observed salespeople being extremely proactive when a sale is in the offing, but then reverting to reactive mode a few months later when they have spent their commission!

If we really do want what the title of this book promises, now, more than ever, we need to take the initiative. If we don't, someone else will and they'll take our customer into the bargain. The old maxim that 'absence makes the heart grow fonder' is untrue when it comes to sales success. A more appropriate saying for salespeople who are reactive would be 'out of sight, out of mind.'

Seize the day

What would have happened to the western world had Winston Churchill not 'seized the day' in being proactive in his approach to Hitler, rather than reactive as with Neville 'Peace in our Time' Chamberlain? Almost certainly, I wouldn't have been writing this book. Some may have welcomed this, but the ability to **anticipate** in any area of life is priceless and distinguishes outstanding performers.

Look at your handwriting. Trust me, I'm a salesman. If you are a right-hander, does it slope backwards, stay upright or slope forward? If you write right-handed and your writing slopes to the left, it often means that you are someone who tends to live in the past, rather than looking to the future.

If this describes you, unless there is some sound physiological reason why you can't write with a forward slope, deliberately make yourself write this way and you will find it may change your way of seeing things. I know it works because I made this same observation to a close friend: it really challenged his thinking and he recognised in himself a tendency to look backwards, like his handwriting. His wife, on seeing a sample of his new forward-slope writing, immediately exclaimed that it was much clearer.

Initiative without empathy spells disaster

Too much initiative can be counter-productive. Richard Boyatzis, author of The Competent Manager, tells of the Vice President of Marketing at a large US company who discovered that one of his salesmen was finding it hard to close a sale with a large major customer.

On his own initiative, the senior executive phoned the company and set up a meeting, telling the salesman to meet him there the next day. They made the sale but the poor salesman was felt made to look foolish. Feeling he had been humiliated in front of his client, the salesman complained and his two immediate line-managers sent angry messages to the insensitive Vice President, stating that he had exceeded his brief, having gone over their heads in humiliating their employee.

The warning had no effect and the pattern continued for two years. The emotionally unintelligent senior executive acted in the same high-handed way with other sales staff, until the Company's president, concerned about a decline in sales, blamed it on the former's demoralisation of the sales force. He issued his Vice President with an ultimatum: take a demotion to regional sales manager – or leave.

The moral of the story? Initiative without emotional intelligence, a lack of basic awareness of the effects of our actions on others, can be a recipe for disaster.

Many years ago I sold business computers and the receptionist at my company, having heard that my father was mentally ill, decided to take the initiative in offering comfort. "It's horrible when they go bonkers, isn't it?" she said memorably and although her initiative was admirable, her clumsy comments displayed a total lack of empathy. It would have been better had she said nothing.

Why is Optimism so important?

There is sound empirical evidence that optimism and sales success are closely linked: classic studies were done by Martin Seligman, a University of Pennsylvania psychologist, on how optimism dramatically increased sales productivity. At MetLife, a large US Insurance Company, he found that optimists sold 29% more insurance in their first year than their pessimistic peers; a staggering 130% more in their second year!

Great Expectations

What you **expect** is so important. If you are reading this book and expecting that nothing will change, that the sales success you desire will always prove beyond your grasp, chances are that it will be a self-fulfilling prophecy and, indeed, nothing will change. We get what we expect and most of us expect far too little.

If you need help with expectations, speak to your partner or a close friend, someone who you know will be positive. Feed off the affirmation of others. Seek out those who believe in you, who see your good qualities – probably clearer than you do. Use any weapon you can to boost your expectations, if necessary a notch at a time.

If one studies the lives of great achievers in all walks of life, often a common theme is a parent or grandparent who planted high expectations in them from an early age, who showed a lot of faith in the individual.

Anita Roddick points to her mother as being the outstanding influence on her from childhood, telling her to dream big dreams and have high expectations... "be special", she would say, "be anything but mediocre." Her Uncle Henry also reassured her mother about Anita, saying there was "something crazy" about the little girl but that she would go on to great things.

Let High Achievers inspire you

Can I please urge you to read one or two biographies of high achievers: I promise they will inspire and motivate you to dream bigger dreams, have much higher expectations. In many cases, an individual will have had to overcome considerable adversity and negative circumstances to reach their goals.

Perhaps we also need to remember that, in the UK, the culture is somewhat different to the US. I talked earlier about Achievement Drive and that it was no accident that many of the world's top global entrepreneurs were American.

It is more difficult to be outstandingly successful in Great Britain, because as a nation we do enjoy a good whinge (are we ever happy with the weather?) and there is a prevailing mood of cynicism, which sometimes results in apathy. Whenever I hit Heathrow's tarmac from a trip abroad, I am immediately struck by the prevailing pessimism (Q: How are you? A: Could be worse) which may not be fertile soil for success, especially in sales.

There is something very American about optimism, a 'frontier ideology' inherited from the earliest settlers that doesn't translate so well into other cultures. In research done amongst top executives in a Global food and drinks company, for example, optimism was a sound predictor of star performance in the United States – but not in Europe or Asia.

Mary Fontaine, MD of the Hay/McBer Innovation and Research Centre, confirms this – *"In many Asian countries, like Japan, Taiwan and India, the can-do-attitude is seen as too bold or individualistic. In these cultures, optimism typically manifests itself in more low-key ways, with the attitude 'this is a very difficult challenge, and I'm trying, even though I may not be able to do it'. You don't hear people saying, "I know I can do it, I know I'm good". And in Europe, what Americans see as optimism can simply seem like arrogance."*

Robin Williams played the part of a teacher in the hit movie *'The Dead Poets Society'*. On the first day of school, he takes his class of boys into the hallway to look at pictures of past, now dead, graduates of the school. He motivates them to excel in life with these words:

"Step forward and see these faces from the past. They were just like you are now. They believed they were destined for great things. Their eyes are full of hope. But you see these boys are now fertilising daffodils. If you listen close, they whisper their legacy to you. Lean in.. what do you hear?

Seize the day, boys. Make your lives extraordinary."

Sanitary needs in Selsey

I can hear you mumbling under your breath "Mellor doesn't understand how tough things are", "What does he know, it's easy for him to say all this." You want some true Confessions? Ok, here goes.

In 1982, I had undergone counselling for depression and anxiety, following a series of casual jobs from which I was sacked with monotonous regularity. I only lasted a month frying cheeseburgers on Littlehampton seafront (they were awful), three months as a publicist for a rock festival (I upset an influential colleague), six months as a barman (too slow).

Prior to 1983, I had been a professional musician for six years, playing in bands, producing albums, doing session work, running my own record label, being moderately successful. Now things were awful. No money, living in a small house in Selsey, West Sussex where the elderly ladies we rented from would take pity on us, emptying the electricity meter and giving us the money back.

One evening they knocked on the door with some toilet rolls, not knowing that we had been using old copies of the West Sussex Gazette for the same purpose. God moves in mysterious ways....

"You'll find this a bit softer, dear."

I was at rock bottom. Waiting to see my optician in his waiting room in Littlehampton, I chanced upon a magazine advertising for Financial Services salesmen and the rest is, as they say, history.

What was the turning point? I had got used to a cycle of failure and so my expectations were zero. My self-confidence was shattered and I was very diffident about accepting the job, because I hadn't worked in the Investment profession since the late 60s. The turning point came when my boss Derek

Gardiner began to raise my expectations and I started to believe that I could once again be successful.

If optimism can be the turning point for me, it can be the same for you. Remember, it is not the circumstances, but the way we respond to circumstances, that is important. Repeat after me, *"There is no such thing as the wrong weather, only the wrong clothes."*

Chapter Eighteen

EMPATHY

—•◦❦◦•—

Empathy is the 'Jewel in the Crown' of Emotional Intelligence. If I had to name just one quality that sets the star salesperson apart from the good or excellent, it is **empathy**. There are many good, some excellent salespeople without this quality, but those who have it, in combination with the other qualities we have been discussing, will go right to the top.

Why is it so important? Because we all have a very deep need to be understood. Given this, our clients feel most comfortable with those who truly understand them and their needs and this translates into top sales performance.

What is empathy?

The Concise Oxford Dictionary tells us that it is 'the power of projecting one's personality into (and so fully comprehending) the object of contemplation'. Any the wiser? No, nor me.

Daniel Goleman knows a thing or two about empathy, so let's see if he can help us. *"Sensing what others feel **without their** *saying so captures the essence of empathy"* is a superb definition and one that we can use as our starting point.

As Sigmund Freud observed – and he also knew a thing or two, not all of it worth knowing – *"Mortals can keep no secret. If their lips are silent, they gossip with their fingertips; betrayal (ie. of their feelings) forces its way through every pore"*.

Heard of Stephen R. Covey? He wrote the bestseller 'The 7 Habits of Highly Effective People', which has sold over 10 million copies worldwide. One of the 7 habits focuses on empathy and he says *"If I were to summarise in one sentence the single most important principle in interpersonal relations, it would be this: **Seek first to understand, then to be understood."***

Social radar

I would go so far as to say that if you only come away with one topic from this book which 'sticks' and you want to work on, make sure it is this. It is both foundational and fundamental. Empathy begins inside and is, if you like, our social radar. Others will often not tell us in words how they really feel. Instead, they will tell us by their facial expression, body language, tone of voice or in other non-verbal ways.

For example, especially in western cultures, we make eye contact, whilst in the east it may be considered rude for a student to make direct eye contact with his professor: deference and respect would dictate that she lower his eyes. In the west, if someone will not make eye contact with you it is an almost sure sign that something is wrong – either the individual is cross with you or has something to hide.

Empathy is all about picking up non-verbal cues, so vitally important in selling that I cannot emphasise it enough. Patrick O'Brien, Vice president of Sales at Johnson Wax, comments *"the best approach is to have a deep understanding of a buyer's business and needs and objectives, listening to hear what is important for the customer's success. It has been one of the fundamentals of sales success for the last century."*

Rapport

O'Brien continues *"...Our sales stars have the ability to balance the world of fact with the interpersonal world. The sales profession has gone from rapport selling to number-based sales; the field has been shifting from the traditional, social sales skills to a model of managers who work their numbers, not their contracts; but you have to balance these. You need the interpersonal side."*

As a starting point, empathy requires the ability to read another's emotions; at the highest level – especially in sales – it means responding to a person's unspoken feelings and needs. You will remember that an earlier chapter was called Knowing me, Knowing you and it is no accident that the words are in that order. In order to understand others, we need to understand ourselves first: without the ability to gauge our own moods and feelings, we will be hopelessly out of touch with the emotions of others.

As is so often the case when considering a particular skill, its absence has much to teach us. A lack of empathy, when taken to extremes, will manifest itself in autism, with the attendant distress for parents and children alike. However, we all know people who are emotionally 'tone deaf', the Saloon Bar bore (or boor) who elbows into a conversation spouting dogmatic opinions, never for a second pausing to find out where others 'are at' and making instant enemies into the bargain.

One can observe children in the playground at primary school who don't pick up crucial cues (and clues) for social interaction when they want to join a game: instead just barging in and disrupting it. More socially adept children will wait and watch, tuning into the game first and then picking an opportune moment to slip naturally into the proceedings.

Death & Voids Dept

I have on my files in the Office a delicious example of *corporate* lack of empathy. A Client of mine, we shall call her Mrs Thomas, was required to write to Scottish Widows' Death & Voids Department to find out further details about her recently deceased husband's Investment Bond. I bet that cheered her up no end.

"Death and Voids Department – how may I help...?"

Individuals who lack empathy have great difficulty in making anything other than surface relationships. Now do you begin to see why I stated earlier that empathy was so important? If a salesman can't make relationships, he will never be successful: it's as basic as that.

No empathy = no relationships = no customers = failure!

Salespeople who are naturally empathic will automatically and subconsciously pick up cues from the client, adjusting to his/her movements and postures, rate of speaking, vocal pitch and mood. This mutual mimicry is subconscious: when we see a happy face (or a sad one), it elicits a similar emotion in us, albeit subtly. To the degree that we adopt facial expression, posture and pace of our clients, we start to live in their 'emotional space' and start to feel emotional attunement.

Fast forward from theory into 21st century western society. Remember the millions of affluent consumers hankering after old-fashioned service confronted at every turn by a machine, which so often becomes the master, not the slave?

Never trust a machine to do what you can do a million times better

One priceless asset you have which a machine can never have, is empathy. Resist Management's calls for each member of the salesforce (ie. you) to be armed with a lap-top at point of sale, because you and your client will be forced to obey the wretched machine's protocols and in any event it will go wrong. Sorry techno-nerds, I will argue this point to the shedding of blood.

How many computer-assisted(?) sales presentations have been hi-jacked because the stupid machine packed up/couldn't interface properly/blew up/delete as appropriate? In my experience, dozens, and yes, I do feel strongly about this topic. Technology has no emotions and in a profession where empathy is vital, don't allow machines to interfere with the precious face to face relationship with your customer, founded on empathy.

Don't get me wrong: there are some situations where the use of computers in a sales presentation is essential, especially with highly technical subjects. But we already know that buying decisions are almost 100% emotional: a machine is likely to get in the way of, rather than assist, the decision-making process.

How can we improve our empathy?

By now, I hope you can see why empathy is such a precious commodity, an essential item in the salesman's toolbox. Without torturing the analogy too far, it is like the spanner which unlocks a customer's decision-making faculties – and wallet. Some of the suggestions I will make may seem a little strange and 'off the wall', but do please bear with me. They have worked for me and I believe can work for you.

In the male-dominated world of sales, there is little room for sensitivity and feelings. When we are under pressure to meet sales targets in tough times, time is at a premium, and surely all our energies need to be focused on earning the dough. No. If we are already failing – or at least struggling – doing more of the same and thereby 'grooving in' bad habits will make matters worse, surely? I believe so and would suggest that you press the pause button for a moment...

Re-awaken your feelings

When was the last time you did something creative? Read a good book, watched a moving play, learnt or played a musical instrument, listened to great music? Now I'm not suggesting that we all become earnest types in belted raincoats reading Proust before breakfast. But I am advocating that you take time to re-awaken those areas of your life where your emotions will be engaged and released.

Empathy is not something you can merely learn from a textbook. It is a quality rooted in the emotions and if your own are well hidden, maybe repressed, it will prove very difficult to make one great leap into full blown empathy within 24 hours. So many of us are so used to a hectic, driven life-style that we have *absolutely no idea how we actually feel*. If this is so, how can we possibly have any comprehension of how our customers feel?

As with most things, recognising that we have a problem means that we are at least 50% of the way to solving it. Getting back in touch with our own emotions is essential and we need to find ways of stimulating what may be a dormant area. That is why music and art therapy is so popular and successful with autistic children: it is a way of helping them to develop sensitivity, assisting them in getting in touch with their own feelings. Once they understand themselves better, this will spill over into their understanding of, and sensitivity to, other people.

Learn to spend time with yourself, enjoying your own company. Take time to smell the roses. Slow down. Stop burying your feelings in frenetic over-activity. Don't feel you have to go to the pub. Somewhere in an attic there is probably a guitar, or a Rolf Harris painting course which has gathered dust for years. Something in you wanted to be creative, but you never had the time. You probably have unfulfilled dreams, like me as a lad of 13 wanting to learn piano. Well I did it, admittedly a bit late, but better late than never.

Allow your memory to drift back to earlier years. See if you can remember a tune which is evocative, which reminds you of an especially happy time. Remember how you felt. If there are situations coming back to you that caused you pain, have a good cry. Release your emotions. If you've been going through a rough time, the chances are that you haven't allowed yourself time for such luxuries. But you owe it to yourself (and incidentally your clients)to get in touch with your feelings.

Empathy = better relationships = more sales = more fulfilment.

Chapter Nineteen

SOCIAL SKILLS

Oh dear, he is going to tell us which knife and fork to use at an executive luncheon and that we should always stand up when a lady enters the room. Before you ask for your money back, please be assured that social etiquette is not what I'm going to talk about.

Social skills in selling are closely linked with empathy, and I will subdivide them into two main areas ease of reference:

(1) Relationship building

(2) Communication skills and persuasion

(1) Relationship building

You may remember my assertion that a salesman who is unable to build relationships will never be successful. It is as simple as that. It is true that the assistant at the supermarket doesn't need highly developed skills in this area in order to sell cans of baked beans. The fact that you don't especially like the forecourt attendant at the local petrol station may not prevent you going back. However, over a period of time you may well use another garage where the attendants are more pleasant.

However, when we are selling more important and expensive goods or services, this skill is vital. "People buy from people" is such a hackneyed phrase that we almost discard it because it's elbow patches are so worn; the fact it is, despite technology's inexorable march forward – or maybe because of it – the ability to build relationships is priceless.

In today's tough times, retaining customers through solid, secure relationships may well be the difference between success and the DSS.

In the affluent west, although we might not say so for fear of political incorrectness, there is a popular notion that our Society is infinitely superior to the less developed nations. True, we may well enjoy a better material standard of living but at a real human cost: breakdown of relationships. There are vast sociological treatises on the subject but take as an example the south east of England. It is full of affluent but lonely old people, whose visit to the corner-shop three times a day may be motivated more by the need for relationship than another bottle of milk!

Our obsession with speed and convenience has led to more and more major shopping areas locating on the outskirts of towns and cities, with the result that the heart of our communities has been clinically removed and not replaced. We all have a basic human need for relationship. Adam needed Eve as a companion, primarily for relationship as well as the, ahem, reproductive aspect.

Michael Schluter and David Lee, co-authors of 'The R Factor' (Hodder & Stoughton), go so far as to say "Loneliness. Violence. Insecurity. Such things are so familiar we think them inevitable.

They are not. They arise because Western society is undermining relationships, which are the foundation of both democracy and the market economy. Relationships are more than the motif for glossy magazines. They are the links which hold society together".

One of the first people to identify the importance of relationships in sales and marketing was Theodore Levitt, Professor of Business Administration at Harvard, in the 1980s. He declared that *"a Company's most precious asset is its relationship with its customers"*. Notice he didn't say that customers were the most precious asset, but the *relationship* with those customers. Professor Levitt continues... *"Relationship management is a special field; it is as important to preserving and enhancing the intangible asset known as goodwill as is the management of hard assets. The sale merely consummates the courtship, at which point the marriage begins."*

In my travels to India and Africa, despite poverty and lack of material comforts, people on the whole seem happier. Why? Because they still understand the importance of relationships. Some Indian friends of mine looked at me with blank faces when I mentioned Rest Homes in the UK. Because family relationships have not broken down as in the West, it is taken for granted that children look after their parents in old age and the notion of a rest home is quite foreign (literally) to them.

How do we build good customer relationships?

OK Laurie, you've beaten me into submission. I agree that building good relationships with clients is essential: how do I enrol in your Relationships Charm School? Well, just recognising that our customers have a basic human need for relationship with us is a good start.

I still play Sunday Club Cricket and recently a player from the opposing team came up to me and asked for a chat. I have known and played against Ken for years and all that time, unbeknown to me, I had been developing a business relationship with him. As we wandered around the boundary, warm English beer in hand, he told me he would have half a million pounds to invest in the next 12 months. Because he had got to know me and trusted me, the business was mine.

People like to do business with those they like, know and trust. More sales are made through good relationships than any number of advanced techniques or slick psychological trickery. I do recognise, though, that there is a great deal of pressure on salespeople to 'hit their numbers' and reach sales targets. This can often lead us, almost subconsciously, to keep trying to find new clients to make new sales, neglecting our existing customers.

Don't neglect existing clients

The British Institute of Management did a recent survey on 'why customers quit', which discovered that 68% of customers are lost 'because of an attitude of indifference towards the customer'. It concluded 'the average Company spends six times more to attract new customers than it does to keep existing ones. Yet customer loyalty in most cases is worth ten times the price of a single purchase'.

Many salespeople have 'diamonds under their feet' which get trampled in the rush for new clients, where more attention to their existing customers would reap rich rewards. When you close a sale, it can be tempting to heave a sigh of relief and assume that the end has arrived. In fact, all that has happened is that the 'prospect' phase of the sales process has ended, and the customer phase has begun.

Building long-term relationships is hard work because often it will involve doing things that, in themselves, don't actually earn you any money. Personal contact is the key. It is so easy for a new customer to become just another name and address on a mailing list, sent standard mail-shots year after year, with no personal contact.

I remember donating a small sum of money to a charity and then being bombarded with repeated requests for further donations. Not once did a representative of the charity have the gumption to telephone me and express their thanks. Had they done so, they would have got far more out of me, to put it bluntly. Needless to say, I never gave to that particular charity again.

We mustn't lose sight of the fact that our clients are not just database entries: they are *people*. Sending birthday and Christmas cards to our clients may seem a tired gesture, but it is always appreciated. Being genuinely interested in the customer's family, his interests and aspirations is all part of building relationships. We do this as a matter of course with family and friends and it is no different in Business.

Ken Lloyd: *"Remember that during the sales process, you devoted a great deal of attention to understanding your prospect's needs and ideally you have sold a product that meets them. That is not where your prospect's needs end, however. After all, some of your prospect's needs were focused on being provided with product support, advice, education, information and responsiveness.*

To build a long-term working relationship with your customer, you need to meet these needs, and this is the point where customer service will play a central role. After all, where do you think the expression 'servicing the account' comes from?"

Being pro-active is essential. You acted as a partner and colleague during the sales process and that is how you should act after the sale. I have lost count of the number of times I have acquired a new client, simply because he or she was clearly not 'looked after' by a competitor; I am sure you can think of examples yourself. But it is so short-sighted, because all the energy and effort that went into turning that prospect into a customer is dissipated, because a long-term relationship was not built.

Use a number of different communication channels. *Adapt to your customer's preferred method of communication.* If your client has made it clear that he prefers literature through the post, don't e-mail him a 90 page unit trust brochure in full colour as an attachment, which takes him an hour to download plus a new printer cartridge. *Using your new-found empathy, think of the effect on your client rather than how much more convenient it is for you.*

Yes, it does happen, because despite repeated requests, my otherwise efficient sales consultant from a well-known Insurance Company will insist on e-mailing me rain-forests, although I have already written several times to say I prefer stuff via the post. This lack of emotional intelligence and listening skills have already cost the company a lot of business.

Networking

An essential aspect of building relationships, this has been going on for centuries but has only surfaced under this name in the past 15–20 years or so. Although it may seem a little cold and calculating, there is no doubt that networking is important. People skilled at networking often mix their professional and private life and it may not be for everybody.

One of the benefits of building relationships via networks is the reservoir of goodwill and trust that is created. Friendships with a commercial purpose, if you will. The networks of top sales performers are not accidental; they are carefully constructed and fellow networkers included 'in the loop' because of a particular skill, or perhaps access to others. What cements a networked relationship is not so much physical proximity – although that helps – so much as pyschological closeness.

Jeffrey Katzenberg is one of the three founders of the Hollywood creative outfit Dreamworks SKG and a Networker par excellence. He has three dedicated secretaries continuously making telephone calls, probing and searching the entertainment industry for contacts, telephoning the hundreds of movers and shakers he stays in touch with as a matter of routine. All this activity keeps his relationships alive and vital, so that when the business need comes along, he can call on them 'seamlessly', pin down a deal.

Face to Face contact vital

Although e-mail, letters, fax and telephone are all important, there is simply no substitute for face-to-face contact in building relationships. Don't fall into the trap of automatically assuming that your Client's preferred method of contact is the same as yours: you might be quite happy to receive 126 e-mails a day, when your client is crying out (maybe literally) for a business discussion over a cup of coffee. If you don't know which channel of communication your client prefers, ask him!

Remember, also, that you are unlikely to get recommendations and referrals unless you are face to face with your customer: very rarely have I had a referral via the post or telephone. You may have had different experiences, but there is nothing like actually being there in person to act as a visual aid, to stimulate your client's memory that he was going to put you in touch with his cousin Tom.

When we have bad news to communicate to a customer, the automatic human instinct is either to delay doing it, get someone else to do it or write or e-mail. Wherever possible, deliver the bad news face to face. Nothing cements a relationship more than the salesperson who has the courage to go in person. Believe me, your clients will respect you for it and realise that you are there for them in the bad times, as well as the good.

In my business, we produce an Annual Valuation Statement, as part of our service. When the figures look bad, I try whenever possible to deliver the offending document in person. Many of my colleagues think I'm certifiable, lamb to the slaughter, etc.

Interestingly though, I've found that even though the first five minutes can be sticky, the psychology of the meeting is such that my reservoir of goodwill is greatly enhanced with the client. Being there in person means I can absorb the flack first-hand and the client is far less likely to jump ship and go to another adviser. In selling, absence certainly does not make the heart grow fonder.

I am going to leave the last word on building relationships to D. W. Cottle, from his book *'Client-Centred Service: How to keep them coming back for more:'* *"relationship management keeps them coming back – again and again"*. **He estimates that companies offering a high quality of service are twice as profitable as others.**

(2) Communication Skills & Persuasion

It may come as no surprise that Bill Gates' preferred method of communication is e-mail. Gates is no salesman (and that's un understatement) – he doesn't have to be because his Microsoft products are so good and you are probably using his software as we speak.

Assuming, though, that you and I still have to sell our products or services, what are communication skills? Why are they so important in selling? What about selling on the telephone? I've heard about NLP – is it for me?

What are Communication Skills?

Communication skills are closely linked with other qualities such as emotional intelligence and empathy.

Remember that communication is two-way: it involves both talking and listening. Remember also that earlier I said that selling was 80% listening and 20% talking. If this is true, then it has profound implications for how we approach the subject. Outside of selling you can be a great communicator but a lousy listener; within the industry, being a great listener is essential to effective communication.

So, hopefully we agree that communication is not just talking: it is a two-way process which involves both the giving and receiving of information. If we have described in agonisingly tortuous detail everything about the product we are selling, but the client suffers from mental overload, effective communication has not taken place.

Effective communication only takes place when the message we have transmitted is the same as the message the customer has received. When the client looks blank, *don't just pile on more information*: she will switch off, if she hasn't already done so. This is one of the commonest mistakes in selling: if only we can say one more thing, we know that we can make the client understand!

Communication skills are therefore those qualities we need to ensure that our customers have really understood – within their own frame of reference and in language they understand – what we have tried to communicate. All the empathy and social skills in the world will not make up for the inability to communicate effectively.

Why are these skills so important in selling?

So often one can see how important a skill is when it is absent. I am sure we have all had our computer go wrong. The chap comes to fix it and you don't understand a word he has said. Why? Because you're dim? Surely not. You would probably say something like 'he speaks a different language' and if effective communication only depended on talking, then why wasn't the computer boffin successful?

Because he is used to dealing with technology, he tends to treat his customers like machines and never actually **asks** them if they have understood and received his transmitted message. Perhaps he is secretly aware that you haven't understood what he's saying, but also knows that he lacks the communications skills to help you understand.

You may be old enough to remember the TV sitcom *'The Rise & Fall of Reginald Perrin'*, where Perrin's boss C.J. used a regular catchphrase *"you're talking my sort of language, Reggie"*. That's what we need to learn as salespeople – to talk the client's language. We will only learn his language by listening. If we want him to talk, we ask questions. I hope this is not overly simplistic, but in tough times it is easy to forget the basics.

Ask open-ended questions and listen to the answers, jotting them down. This will reinforce in the client's mind that you really are listening. It never ceases to surprise me when I am being sold to how little the salesman will write down; often I will ask him to jot something down just to be sure in my own mind that he really has been listening! Open-ended questions typically start with "who". "what", "how", "where" and "when", rather than questions that can merely be answered with a yes or no.

There is a whole body of literature on communication styles and we don't have room here to touch on more than the basics. If your client is a 'thinker', ask him "what do you think about xyz", if a 'feeler', "how do you feel about xyz". Don't be afraid to ask questions – your customer will not be offended, quite the opposite. Don't be afraid to allow the Client to seemingly control the interview; in fact, you are actually controlling it because of the questions you ask and your client will lead you to the things that are most important to him.

Be careful with the use of the question "why". It can come across as accusatory or judgmental: better to ask "how do you mean?" which means the same but is much softer.

When describing the product or service you are selling, use stories, paint pictures. These can be much more powerful than graphs, charts, technical specifications, etc. Make them short and punchy and relevant to both the client and the situation. Never be tempted to bring out your favourite gag – especially a dubious one you've just heard – just because you find it funny: it may be totally inappropriate and kill the presentation stone-dead.

Chapter Twenty

DESSERT

NLP

In the ever-growing literature of selling, Neuro Linguistic Programming – NLP to you and me – has, in the last ten years, become the Julia Roberts of Sales. Alluring, beautiful and with big lips. Actually the analogy doesn't totally work, but you get the gist. You may detect in my tone a slight reservation about the subject, and you'd be right. I do have a certain ambivalence towards it which I examine in greater detail later.

There is no doubt, however, that this book would be incomplete without an introduction to the subject, especially if it's new to you. I would also say that in the right hands, NLP has much to teach us and contains some exceptional and valuable insights.

There are two books I would especially recommend and which I draw upon, although not exclusively, in this section: *'Selling with NLP'* by Kerry Johnson and *'Successful Selling with NLP'* by Joseph O'Connor & Robin Prior.

I'll kick off by letting Kerry Johnson speak for himself, from the back cover of his book:

"Kerry Johnson reveals the hidden techniques that top sales professionals unconsciously use and how you can master these simple but profound techniques by using NLP, as series of powerful discoveries about behaviour, communication and trust.

The book will teach you to become a detective of human behaviour, to reinforce the trust you have gained and communicate with your clients on deeper, ever more subtle, levels. Using both verbal and physical skills, you will learn how to pace your sales meetings.

Every salesperson will discover how to establish rapport with ease and assurance, listen to clients more effectively, turn objections into approval, and discover a client's buying strategy in minutes. Selling with NLP also contains charts, diagrams and quizzes, as well as a twenty-one-day programme which guarantees that every reader will be successfully employing Johnson's techniques within weeks."

Johnson's Company motto:

"If you can see John Smith through John Smith's eyes, you will sell John Smith what John Smith buys". This is a good starting point for our brief precis of how NLP can enhance our sales performance.

Geoffrey Gray, Regional Director at TSB Ltd and a former valued colleague of mine at International Life Insurance, says in his foreword to O'Connor & Prior's book *'Selling is an honourable profession'* – *"NLP provides us with a framework to recognise important things within ourselves and the way we relate to others. I have used it at TSB and it works"*.

Feargal Quinn, Founder of Irish Supermarket chain Superquin, says *"One of the reasons I enjoyed this book, and why*

I think it will be useful to anyone engaged in any kind of selling, is because of the strong emphasis Joseph O'Connor & Robin Prior put on building a relationship with customers. The person who nurtures customer relationships by responding to their needs is building an income stream that will continue to grow over many years".

NLP and Empathy are close bed-fellows, different perspectives on what is essentially the same massive subject. Where empathy looks at customer behaviour from an essentially human, intuitive viewpoint, NLP approaches it more clinically and physiologically, even scientifically

In the late 1970s, research was being done in the University of California at Santa Cruz, on an exciting new area of psychology called Neuro Linguistic Programming. The founders of NLP, John Grinder and Richard Bandler, studied the working methods of therapists who were especially successful with their clients. All had one thing in common: the successful therapists were all superb at gaining their clients' trust.

Kerry Johnson, a former professional tennis player, decided to see whether the secrets of NLP could be applied in sales situations. Grinder & Bandler gave him the answer as to why trust developed in some therapeutic situations, but not in others. We all have different ideas of reality – ways in which we perceive the world – and we can only really trust people who look at the world the way we do.

Johnson spoke to the top sales performers who seemed to get their clients to buy without really trying. He asked them the secrets of their success and they merely shrugged their shoulders, saying that it was down to years of experience. Then he began to apply the dynamics uncovered by NLP as he observed these top performers in action, and began to see clearly what was happening and why.

Be careful

He goes on to say "selling can be magic, but a magic based on understanding specific buying patterns and rules of sales psychology. As a matter of fact, I guarantee that you will double your sales in the first year".

Most NLP text-books will then go on to discuss topics such as these:

● People have three basic methods of perceiving the world: visual, auditory or kinesthetic.

● Visuals are those who see the world

● Auditories hear the world

● Kinesthetics feel the world.

● Once the salesperson understands a client's 'mental map' he adapts his style accordingly.

● Eye movements: the three categories above show what they are thinking via different eye movements.

● An example of the above is that an auditory (one who 'hears' the world) when looking to the right, is probably thinking about future information (eg. "I wonder what my wife will think later when she finds out I bought this").

● Mirroring- matching body movements.

● Matching voice patterns and pacing.

● Using the Customer's language.

● Re-framing: taking a negative situation and turning it into something positive.

I hope this brief introduction has whetted your appetite to read more on the subject. Note the use of the term 'Programming' in the subject and that Johnson refers to the new 'technology' of selling in his book. I said earlier that I had my reservations. I have an inbuilt distaste for anything which may smack of manipulation, using mimicry and pretence in an attempt to control people, especially in sales situations.

You may say that clients cannot be manipulated, they have free will and therefore will do what they want to do. Probably true of the majority, but vulnerable widows in their 80s, for example, are capable of being manipulated. I dislike Johnson's phrase 'the technology of selling' in the same way as I dislike the fact that my degree in Sociology (BSc Hons) is a science degree. People are NOT a science!

Please don't misunderstand me: I believe NLP has many fascinating and useful insights, but handle with care.

USE OF THE TELEPHONE

You will note from the index that I have devoted a fair bit of space to this topic. This is because (a) it is often neglected in sales textbooks and (b) if we are really struggling, effective use of the telephone is probably the quickest way to turn things round fast.

I recognise that there may be a real urgency about turning our sales performance around and that we need to see results fast. That is why I have devoted a disproportionate amount of space to the subject.

With only a certain number of hours in the day, it makes sense right now to maximise our use of the telephone. The telephone is certainly a 'warmer' medium for making contact than e-mail and fax; much of what I said about communication skills apply to use of the telephone, the obvious difference being that you cannot see your customer/prospect.

Perhaps you don't know quite know where to start. Maybe you can identify with American movie star Douglas Fairbanks Jr., who once started an important lecture by saying *"I feel like a mosquito in a nudist colony. I look around and know its wonderful to be here, but I don't know where to begin"*.

As I was doing my research for this book, it struck me that there are few books devoted to the use of the telephone, certainly disproportionate to the amount we use it. Several of the best-selling titles on selling don't even have 'Telephone – use of' in the index, let alone a chapter devoted to the topic.

This puzzled me but I came to the the conclusion that (a) it is a difficult subject and (b) there is confusion over the role that use of the phone plays in selling.

Why is it a difficult subject? Surely everyone knows how to use it? You pick it up, you dial the number. If only it were that simple: but we are talking about one of the most powerful weapons in the salesman's armoury and this is why I am devoting a whole section to it. My study of successful salespeople over the years leads me to the firm conclusion that all top performers, without exception, are masters of its use.

Let's look first at why you might be finding use of the telephone difficult.

Climate of gloom

It's hard to keep positive when half an hour earlier you were watching GM TV with its daily diet of bad economic news, war in the middle east, another Chief Executive resigning, all delivered in a strangely cheerful voice by Fiona Phillips. After all, we're only human and not immune to the climate of genteel negativity that hovers over the British Isles.

When we pick up the phone to make that first sales call, we need to deliberately focus on positives, even to the extent of starting off our call with an upbeat comment about the weather, the daffs are early this year, etc. Emotions are

infectious and people tend to mirror those of others so that if
you are cheerful, the chances are that you will lift the spirits of
your client/prospect.

Hawaiian shirt

When phoning, try wearing a Hawaiian shirt. Yes, I know, silly
but I have found it almost impossible to be depressed and
gloomy if I am wearing such an item. One look in the mirror
will make you smile, then break into a laugh and hey presto,
you're in the right frame of mind. Don't wear it to the
appointment, though.

It's amazing how one little positive can lift our mood and
transform a depressing day into one where we make 4 or
5 appointments.

Fear of Rejection

An old favourite, one identified as long ago as the
Cholmondely-Warner* type Sales Textbooks of the 1950s, but
as relevant now as it was then. Remember if they say no, they
are not rejecting you as a person but just saying "no, I don't
want to buy what you are selling at the moment", or "I don't
want to see you, at the moment". Also, we forget that if we can
change our minds quickly, so do clients and a 'no' this week
may well be a 'yes' next week, simply because our client is in
a different mood.

Persistence is everything. You cannot beat it. I hope these don't
sound like clichés, but when times are tough we have to go
back to basics. Ray Kroc, founder of the McDonalds' empire,
says about persistence:

*"Nothing in the world can take the place of persistence. Talent will
not; nothing is more common that unsuccessful men with talent.
Genius will not; unrewarded genius is almost a proverb. Education*

*Cholmondely-Warner: A stiff upper lip, British type character from
Harry Enfield's TV show.

will not; the world is full of educated derelicts. Persistence and determination alone are omnipotent".

When Africans pray, and see no answers to their prayers, it spurs them on to pray even more forcefully, because their logic tells them that they must be getting closer to the answer! We need the same mind-set when we are prospecting, seeing every 'no' as one step nearer the 'yes'. These are not mind-games, but instead a highly practical way of transforming your attitude towards using the phone.

I've got so much else to do

I'm sure you have, but what are your priorities? Remember back to Not So Clever Trevor, the consultant I mentioned in an earlier chapter, who made his first sales call at 4.47pm after spending the previous 7 hours lighting cigarettes, answering personal correspondence, doing crosswords, poring over junk mail, lighting another cigarette, entering prize draws, feeding and watering an overheated dog in his car, making endless cups of coffee.

Some sales text-books would dignify this behaviour with the term 'Call Reluctance', whereas I would call it sheer stupidity and laziness. Do those activities that earn, or have the potential to earn you money. The rest can, indeed must, wait, if you are to remain solvent.

You may be at this place yourself. If you are, you must earn money and you don't earn money by sales-avoidance activities. Most struggling salesmen could pass a doctorate on Sales Avoidance without breaking sweat, because we start finding other activities which make us feel busy and pretend to be productive. You must break this vicious circle.

If you are starting to bristle at my comments, that's ok, I can take it. Sometimes we need someone else to shake us, to stop us in our tracks and help us confront reality. This is your career, your livelihood, not the Vicar's garden party. Unless you believe in re-incarnation, you reckon that you only have one crack at life and you owe it to yourself – and your family – to pick up the phone.

OK, you've been in detention long enough. Time to move on to look at possible confusion over the role of the telephone in selling.

Why are you picking up the phone?

This may seem a silly question, but what are you trying to achieve with your phone call? It may be that because you are unsure, this is adding to reluctance to pick it up. Are you trying to sell over the phone? Yes and no. Oh dear, more confusion. Not really. I'm sure you have heard it said many times before that you can't really sell anything substantial over the phone, and I pretty much agree with that.

Let's be clear that your purpose in using the phone in prospecting is either to make an appointment, or to give further information which may lead to that appointment. Where many salespeople go wrong – especially if they are under pressure to perform – is to go for the whole shooting-match on the first sales telephone call. If you are selling cars, by all means extol the virtues of the air-conditioning and hand-stitched leather seats (The M.D. has them) but stop selling the car and 'sell' the appointment.

You may think I'm insulting your intelligence, but even gnarled old pros like you and me can forget first principles, faced with a mountain we don't think we can climb. Our emotions play such a powerful part in what we believe we can do; in the same way as our customers make buying decisions largely on emotional factors, it is our emotions which determine whether we believe we can achieve our goals... or not.

How to use the telephone in Selling

Having looked at difficulties, let us look closely at the secrets of success. Emotional intelligence and empathy are qualities that will stand us in good stead when we pick up the phone; everything I have said about really understanding your client also applies in this area. However, since you are not 'eyeball to eyeball' with the customer, you can't observe aspects like body language and, as we shall see, quite a lot of principles from NLP won't apply, since they are based on facial observations.

The fact that the customer can't see us may be an advantage, depending on how ugly we are. In the same way as we will be forming a mental picture of what he/she looks like, the customer will be starting to visualise us. Factors such as accent, tone of voice, what sort of words we use, whether we are polite or smarmy, all combine to create a picture in the client's mind of who we are and what we look like.

Remember, we only get one chance to make a first impression and so our preparation for the call should be thorough. In my days as a Regional Sales Manager, I watched many salesmen making prospecting calls, rushing into conversations without even having the correct papers, eating a cheese sandwich with one hand whilst balancing the phone with the other.

More recently, I had a telephone call from the Managing Director of a newly formed Financial Services Company, trying to recruit me. Although I already knew and liked Colin, he was making the call from what sounded like Starbucks in the middle of London and immediately I switched off. Clearly the call wasn't important to him, with the ear-splitting hiss of the capuccino machine and loud conversations going on around him, so it wasn't important to me! No preparation and no professionalism.

Assuming you have prepared well, how should you approach the call?

GOLDEN RULES

Be considerate

Remember that your prospect or customer is, first and foremost, a human being. You may see her as telephone fodder and just the means to a pay-cheque, but she is, like you, another person with needs and emotions. She may be having a bad-hair day. She may be in the middle of sorting out the kids. She may have just had an argument with her partner, be in a foul mood and the last thing she wants is a voice she may not instantly recognise. If so, she will see you as an annoyance. *Use your empathy – put yourself in her shoes and don't rush the conversation.*

Forget the high octane sales text-books with their 'power lines' and just relate to your customer as one human being to another. First of all, ask if this is a convenient time to call. Obvious? You would have thought so, but the number of times I am telephoned at 6.15 p.m. by a 'market research company' (ha ha), who breeze straight into their robotic pre-written script is countless.

Even if I said I was in the throes of a heart attack, I doubt whether this would alter their spiel. You see, they are not trained to talk to human beings and that is why their success rate is about 0.000000001%. It always will be unless they radically change their approach.

The simple question "is this a convenient time?" is more profound than at first sight. First, it tells the customer you are a caring human being. Second, right at the start you are breaking down the psychological 'distance' between customer and salesman, in effect saying you want to start a business relationship rather than launching into the stereotypical hard sell. So often I have found this engaging of emotions, albeit initially at a surface level, has elicited a positive or even relieved response.

Speak slowly to start with

When you first telephone to introduce yourself, remember you may be one of several sales calls the customer has received over the last fortnight, not to mention the steady stream of leaflets, junk mail, unsolicited faxes and adverts they have received. Don't assume they were just waiting by the phone for your call and immediately know who you are. They are mentally trying to 'place you' in one of two categories: a time-waster or someone they may want to speak to.

So that they can process this information, speak slowly so that they have time to gather their thoughts, 'get their bearings', if you will. Don't be afraid of silence even at the start of the call. Our idea of who we are may be very different from the customer's. Like it or not, we are part of a massive Sales Market-Place, and the customer may have had bad experiences with salesmen in the past.

If the prospect is a little reluctant to talk, I will craftily use a bit of empathy and ask innocently "Am I right in thinking that there is a little reluctance on your part to talk; have you perhaps had a poor experience in the past with a salesman?" Believe me, people will answer the question honestly and you will get advance warning of possible objections.

Don't be too quick to press for an appointment

Yes, that's what I said. There is the Attila the Hun School of Salesmanship which urges recruits to push for an appointment within the first 30 seconds, at any price. Tosh.

Why should anyone in their right mind agree to see you – and all that might entail in terms of perceived obligation – when you are still a total stranger? It's just not logical or reasonable. You are trying to open the relationship, not close the sale (in this case, the 'sale' being getting an appointment).

You can bully people into an appointment, in the same way as you can bully a prospect into a sale, but it is 99.99% certain that (a) they will leave a message on your ansafone, (craftily, after business hours, so they don't have the embarrassment of talking to you) cancelling the appointment, or (b) you will drive the 45 miles to the appointment, tired and harassed and they are out or (c) they are in, but glued to the TV set – which is their way of saying go away.

The trouble is that some sales organisations target their salesmen and tele-sales staff to make a certain number of appointments, so I do understand if you are under pressure in this area. Follow your instinct, though: if someone is really reluctant to see you over the phone, it will be no different in the flesh, despite your Austin Reed suit, cunningly co-ordinated accessories and handbag, lashings of Obsession, charm and personality. And that's just the men.

Don't be too familiar

Although we are trying to build a relationship with our prospect, be very careful not to be presumptuous and call him by his first name. Ideally, wait until they give you permission to use their christian name or, if you judge the moment to be right, ask "would it be all right if I called you John"?

There are cultural differences between the UK and the US on this topic, and if you are reading this in the States then I may be wrong: if so, disregard my advice. But in the UK – and especially amongst the over 50s – using a customer's first name without prior permission will be seen as over-familiar and will get you points deducted.

Go at the right pace – the Client's

I am renowned amongst my colleagues for taking a long time on my initial sales calls – between 15-20 minutes is average. This is only when I have a strong feeling that there is a potential client in the making. If not, I will wrap up the call within the first few minutes in a polite and business-like way. Remember, we don't get paid to have good conversations: we only get paid to have good conversations which lead to business.

Begin to tune in to the Client's pace, speech patterns, accent and 'hot buttons'. Ask loads of open-ended questions, use anecdotes, ask them if they've looked at other products/services they found interesting. Get them talking and they will lead you unerringly to the pot of gold: their perceived need, to which you have the solution.

Make lots of notes about what is important to them

If they say it must be a red car, don't persist in trying to enthuse them about a green one. Make lots of notes about what is important to them. If they say I would like your 125 page colour brochure *through the post*, don't cunningly e-mail it as an attachment. Like me, they probably won't download it and although it may have been convenient for you, if they don't read it there is no point. Just because we may be short of time doesn't mean we can ignore what the prospect wants.

Sorry if I am banging on again about what the **customer** wants, but it does seem rather essential to me.

Use your voice effectively

In the same way as an opera singer's voice is the main 'tool of the trade' so is yours, especially when using the telephone. Because the customer can't see you, he is making his judgment largely based on your voice.

Ken Lloyd again *"Your voice is one of the most valuable tools in selling by phone. You can train it, develop it and build it into an instrument that can make a real difference. Listen to the voices of people who are highly trusted, and then listen to a tape recording of your own voice. Are you doing everything to make your voice interesting, trustworthy and captivating? Are you projecting your words with strength and confidence? The overall tone of your voice is at least as important as the content."*

If you have ever practised a musical instrument, you will know what it takes to get a better sound. Well, as a salesperson, the instrument you are playing is your voice. So, don't forget to practise.

Don't, however, put on a posh or affected voice. Remember Sir Alf Ramsey, Manager of the successful 1966 England World Cup Squad? He tried to disguise a cockney accent with a veneer of sophistication and the result was, in my opinion, awful. People are not stupid and will see through this. Just be yourself, but be the best that you can be.

Ansafone messages

These are more important than you might think. Almost everyone has an ansafone these days and often use them as a 'screening' device, to see whether they want to talk to the caller or not. If you have to leave a message, make it warm, concise, friendly and be open as to the purpose of your call. If your name is David Jones, do not say that Mr Jones called – he didn't, David Jones did. Mr is a title that others give you: I'm not splitting hairs, it's just what is correct.

That first ansafone message is the equivalent of the first pre-approach letter. In essence, you are going to leave a 20–30 second commercial about yourself and your company. Don't garble a name and phone number with machine gun rapidity and remember that even though you are familiar with your name, others won't be. Speak slowly and distinctly. Or is it only me who regularly gets unintelligible messages from fluent martian rhyming-slang speakers, on my ansafone?

Don't hurry

Don't hurry, unless it is clear that the customer doesn't have much time. Swim against the tide: we live in a fast-paced culture where e-mail and the Net are speeding everything up. The trouble is that this process is insidious and we don't realise that we are doing everything at a much faster pace.

Remind your prospect that you know and understand that he is a human being by deliberately slowing the pace; show him you want to make a relationship with him rather than just flogging something and moving on to the next prospect.

I probably am too laid-back in my approach, but I want to demonstrate that I have time for people. I promise you that this relaxed approach will pay dividends, especially amongst older prospects. Without being too folksy, imagine you are talking to them over a garden fence.

Never cold call – use Pre-Approach letters

If you cold call someone without any prior contact, you are placing yourself at a tremendous disadvantage.

I built my 1000+ Client Bank largely through sending out thousands of pre-approach letters, in the early days working well into the night, printing out letters using mail-merge, signing and putting them in envelopes. To be honest, I can't remember making a truly 'cold' call and would strongly recommend that you never do so.

When you call someone 'cold', everything is against you. Using your new found empathy, put yourself in their shoes. What would be your over-riding priority? To get rid of the caller. Why? Because this is an unsolicited telephone call and the British especially do not take kindly to intrusion of their privacy.

If this is how you'd react, it is no different for your prospect. He will feel that you have 'put him on the back foot', will be defensive and will probably not give you a hearing. He may well slam the phone down on you. You have invaded his space and not shown that highly prized British virtue (yes, even now) courtesy.

Despite what your Company may have told you – ie. go to the library, get the local telephone directory and start phoning – I wouldn't bother. It's a waste of time. If your company insist you do this, then leave – if that's their idea of warm leads, I promise you there's no future there.

Sending a 'pre-approach' letter is courteous and gives you a far better chance of a good reception. What is it? A letter introducing yourself, your Company and its products and services, enclosing your business card. Make sure it is only one page long and use a *p.s.*, because research proves that the *p.s.* is usually read first by the recipient.

Make sure you sign it in ink (fountain pen or rollerball is OK) not biro, and take care that your signature is legible. Oh come on Laurie, I didn't pay good money for this book to be lectured about kindergarten stuff. No, you didn't, but because of the pace of life I was talking about earlier, we can all become careless and not realise it.

I receive letters bearing signatures which resemble a tangled ball of wool, the product of a troubled mind. If that's you, change it. Many are unsigned or merely initialled. Call me old-fashioned, but I reckon that's bad manners and from the feedback I receive from clients, they agree.

There are several good books on how to write and use effective sales letters and if you are struggling in this area, you owe it to yourself to invest in one or two. Remember, the pre-approach letter is the first communication your prospect receives from you, so it has to look professional and business-like.

Be easy on yourself

Because often the salesman's lot is a lonely one, there is nobody there to encourage you and say 'well done' when you get an appointment. You have to be your own encourager, your own sales manager if you like.

Break your time down into manageable chunks. If you begin at 9.00am, give yourself a reward at 10.00. If you get an appointment, maybe a bar of chocolate. Three appointments = a giant toblerone. Say to yourself, after another six calls I'll make a cup of coffee. Prospecting on the phone is a lonely job so you need to be good company to yourself.

Pick the best time of day to make your calls. If you are at your best in the morning, make your calls then; if in the evening, the same, but don't forget the over-riding consideration: *when do your prospects prefer that you contact them?*

Working from Home

Having your own dedicated work-space is crucial to your sales performance.

If you are working from home, I know it's difficult, especially with young children – I speak from experience. Ideally you need a room separate to the rest of the house.

Have you ever thought of a shed in the garden? For between £1,000 – £2,000 you can kit yourself out with a pleasant office, with electricity, heat, computer, all your gadgets and hopefully a pleasant view of the garden/window box. If you can afford a bit more, there are several 'garden offices' on the market.

You may have to be firm with your partner and say "sorry, can't pick up the kids from school, I'm working". I'm sure they'll understand, especially if your activities are earning money!

Chapter Twentytwo

THE FORGOTTEN CUSTOMER
– PART TWO

In Part One of The Forgotten Customer, we looked at the major changes in the Sales Marketplace. Here, we look at the future of Customer Service and the impact of Sales Training methods on clients' changing perceptions of Salesmen. As we shall see, Customer Service still has a golden future.

The ideas absorbed from the Sales Training of the last 50 years have had a tremendous influence on selling and by implication on Customers' perceptions of the selling profession. In the same way that the Marketplace has changed, the business of selling, and therefore sales training, has changed enormously in the space of a generation.

The expectations of the customer/consumer have changed drastically but those in charge of sales operations have been very slow to recognise this: analytical ability is not a quality one immediately associates with all sales managers. Some of them are in their fifties and sixties, sometimes promoted beyond their ability.

A classic mistake, especially prevalent in sales, is to promote the best salesman to the position of Sales Manager; often because he has pushed and pushed for it, craving recognition and status. Many of these individuals spent their formative years absorbing the sales ideas and culture which came across the Atlantic from the US... and it shows, even in the early 2000s.

I recently attended a National Sales Convention in London, at which a 'nationally known motivational speaker' held forth for about one and a half hours. It was like going back 30 years into a time-warp. These are some of the notes I made at the time:

Patronising, opinionated.

Bullying, arrogant, 'cringe-making'.

Ill prepared, no research.

Hasn't updated material since the Seventies.

Dandruff on collar; sweating profusely.

One of his special 'Power Lines' (as he called them) which he advocated delegates should use when selling life assurance was to ask the prospect "Do you happen to know the expiry date on your birth certificate?".

Another classic, when encountering resistance from a potential client, was the immortal "Okay, I'll phone back in six months... if you're not there (ie.dead) who should I ask to speak to?"

During the late fifties and sixties, when the new 'theology' of selling was in its infancy, I remember as a boy reading the course notes my father (Sales Manager with Remington) would bring home from sales conferences he attended in the

States. In precis, these were the key ideas underpinning this material:

- selling was an aggressive act which you, the salesman, did to the customer.

- Selling was being made into a science. You could predict customer behaviour and, as long as you pressed all the right buttons, a sale must result.

- Sales *Techniques* became very popular. Close That Sale, 101 Winning Ways to get the order, how to make the Customer say Yes every time were typical headlines for sales courses.

- Although the word Manipulation might not have actually been used, much of the 'theology' underpinning the new sales ethos tacitly inferred the manipulation of the customer. If you have ever stumbled across titles like ' the use of psycho-cybernetics in selling' you will know what I mean.

Is it any accident that the same period saw the birth of the Consumer Rights Lobby to protect the innocent consumer from wolves in three-piece suits? And yet, going back to our Sales Manager in his late 50s or 'National Motivational Speaker' mentioned earlier, so many are even now operating with the sales paradigms they learnt in their formative years.

So far, though, I have related only one side of the story. To suggest that all salesmen are, or were, manipulative and dishonest is to present a lop-sided picture, unfair to the thousands of honest and conscientious salespeople.

My wife tells me of a friend who became a life insurance salesman, because his father died young with no life assurance: the friend saw at first hand how much his mother and the family struggled without adequate financial resources. He needed no further convincing of the merits of the product he was selling.

Many people are actually in the business of selling without realising it. The greengrocer, the newsagent, the restaurant owner – the list is endless – are all selling something, but might be reluctant to be described as salesmen, with the negative connotations that the term might conjure up.

The customer's perception of whether he is dealing with a salesman or not is heavily influenced by the location where the sales interaction has taken place. As we will see, there is a paradox. If the Company representative goes to the customer's home, he will be perceived as a salesman and ironically, although the customer is on his own home territory, he is likely to be more suspicious and on his guard, than if the encounter took place on the salesman's home territory, ie. his shop or office.

I have noticed this in my own business as an Independent Financial Adviser, even in the relatively respectable area of investment advice: clients who come to my Office perceive me differently, like a solicitor or accountant, and are almost deferential at times. Location, or context, is therefore very important in the sales process.

Customer Service – The Future

The Marketplace has changed dramatically over the last forty years: our analysis suggests that Consumers, believing themselves to be Customers, are bewildered and angry at the lack of customer service they receive.

They are sick to death of pressing buttons on a telephone, listening to Tesco's Chill-Out Classics, longing for the golden age of the Man from the Pru and unhurried personal service. Sadly, they are victims of the remorseless drive to cut costs, in which they have been naive accomplices. They haven't realised that you cannot have rock-bottom prices and Rolls Royce service.

Anita Roddick, in her inspiring autobiography *'Body and Soul'* says *"I am still looking for the modern-day equivalent of those Quakers who ran successful businesses, made money because they offered honest products and treated their people decently, gave honest value for money, put more back than they took out and told no lies. This business creed, sadly, seems long forgotten."*

She continues...*"In the old days, the great British retailers may well have been driven by the profit motive but they were also great philanthropists, pillars of society and builders of the community".*

I agree with her sentiments, but think she has overdone the doom and gloom. Her analysis, whilst excellent, overlooks the tens of thousands of conscientious salespeople still passionate about customer service.

I interviewed James Febraro, Restaurant Manager at the world famous Breakers Hotel in Palm Beach, Florida: by reputation, one of the top five hotels in the world. Jim is used to dealing with billionaires, rock stars, movie idols – in short the mega-rich and famous – on a daily basis. I asked him what was the most important quality in dealing with them and without hesitation, he said *"anticipating the needs of our guests".*

He went on to say that *"responsiveness is important – when you sit down to dine a server should immediately come over, but be unobtrusive. The cardinal sin, which annoys me personally if I'm on the receiving end, is if the customer is not acknowledged within 10–15 seconds of entering a restaurant".* Memo to the M.D. at Little Chef.

Over the past couple of years, I have written a monthly column for our in-house Company magazine and Customer Service has been a common theme. In one article, I mention that there will always be a strong demand for face to face Customer Service, no matter how much regulation is thrown at us as salesmen: *"Whether we become AFAs, IFAs or sweet Fas won't alter one iota the strong demand for good, old-fashioned personal service."*

In another column: *"Times are hard. Sometimes it is right to make changes for change's sake if your methods are not producing results; sometimes the methods are right and you simply need to keep on keeping on. Enough of the homespun philosophy. I can only tell you what works for me and it is nothing new. It is called service. If you have no appointments in your diary, go to see clients to review their investments.*

But the valuations are dreadful. Yes, I know... and so does the client. Clients will respect you for confronting difficulties head on and for being there for them when times are bad. They will feel comfortable doing more business with you and giving you referrals.

I speak from experience- not some sales textbook. I know there are tremendous pressures to generate new business – believe me, I've been there, but have lived to tell the tale.

I learnt that the secret was service."

I asked Paddy Ellis, Partner with City Marketing & Motivation, major Events Organisers and corporate hospitality specialists, *how she dealt with a difficult client. Her response: "Defuse the situation with humour, charm and courtesy. Draw alongside him/her, using empathy and stressing that we are here to help, as partners in ensuring your Event is a success."*

Surely the Internet makes personal service redundant?

Granted, buying decisions are now often made over the Internet, but the vast reservoir of information and knowledge available via the web can cause busy people to throw up their hands in frustration and seek face to face customer service.

I think the key word is *busy*. If you are retired and have time on your hands, it is perfectly feasible to do all your research via the internet and buy next year's holiday to Mauritius on line. You can bypass the local travel agents altogether. I think we have to be real and acknowledge that many do make buying decisions on the Net.

As we all know, though, the problem comes when we get stuck (or is it only me?) and the Computer Screen can't answer a question for us, however hard we shout at it. There is no human being on the other end of the modem, and because computers operate on the binary system, they can only answer yes/no questions. If you have a how, what or why type question, you're a bit stuck.

Also, buying products/services using modern technology obliges you to play the role of Do-it-Yourself Administrator as well as Customer, roles that not everyone is happy to combine. Remember back to the D.I.Y Administrator/Customer buying tickets for Virgin Cinema via the automated telephone service. A nightmare.

The rapid expansion of the World Wide Web has expanded the overall market-place. A good example would be books, where the On Line Virtual bookshops provided by the likes of Amazon.com have stimulated customers to visit real bookshops like Waterstones and Ottakars in the UK, and Barnes & Noble in the US. I'm sure the reverse is also true, with visits to real bookshops leading to a cut price purchase via the Net.

If I am right, why doesn't Amazon have hundreds of retail outlets and Waterstone's a sophisticated on-line service, to avoid business being pinched from them by the other? What I am hinting at is that the Net retailers should provide a simple link (no passwords, auntie's maiden name and all that rhubarb) to a human being providing personal service, to ensure that they get the business.

No doubt the accountants will tell me that "the margins won't allow it", but I would always offer personal human service alongside technology. Not either/or, but both/and, if you follow my thinking.

Most people complain that even the simplest of purchases these days are fraught with complexity. When in Sarasota, Florida, recently I asked for a coffee. This was the Assistant's reply:

"Capuccino?... Latte?... Frappucino?... Espresso?... Double Espresso?... Mocha?... Filter?... Kenyan?... Moroccan?... Specialty?... Regular?... Large?... Extra Large?... With cinammon?... With almond?... With chocolate chips?... Do you have a Regular Customer Card?... To drink here or take away?..."

I forget the rest of the questions.

I said to the Assistant "You decide for me", which threw her into a flap; she hadn't understood that my question was a coded message for "this is over-choice, life's too short" and went away sadder but not wiser.

What has this to do with the future of Customer Service? My view is that lightning fast technology and over-choice will stimulate the demand for personal customer service, especially amongst the busy, affluent, middle classes.

It's already happening. The sheer complexity of modern life in the west has given birth to a growing number of individuals and firms who will sort out your personal filing, organise house purchase, fill in forms, wait in queues on your behalf, organise your shopping, administer the cat, etc. They charge between £50 and £100 per hour and are inundated with work. People who can afford to will pay for personal service.

I believe the market is polarising: a growing number of goods and services at the lower end of the market will be purchased via the Net; the higher ticket/higher value goods and services will be bought, in the main, via personal customer service.

Considering a career change?

If you are in sales and thinking about a move into a different industry, my advice would be to look at the 'upper' end of the market. Remember, you have skills that are transferable into almost any sales context.

In retail, for example, no matter how good your customer service skills you will never make much money running a tobacconists: however, using those same skills in a prestige Estate Agency in Hampstead makes a lot of sense.

Working at a High Street furnishers, where selling a £750 three-piece suite will earn you around £7.50 commission on top of your £9000 p.a. basic salary doesn't have a great future: getting a job at David Linley's bespoke furniture showroom in Chelsea, where prices start at £3000 is likely to be better remunerated.

In conclusion

Customer Service still has a great future. Those sales people who swim against the tide of mediocrity and consumerism, who remember that consumers really long to be customers and pampered with personal service, have a golden future.

I'll leave the last word on the subject to Mahatma Gandhi, not someone you immediately associate with selling; however, it should be remembered that before returning to India to fight for independence, he had his own law firm in South Africa.

Here is his take on the subject, as fresh now as when it was written 100 years ago. Why not type it out and put in your office?

> *"A customer is the most important visitor on our premises. He is not dependent on us. We are dependent on him. He is not an interruption in our work. He is the purpose of it. He is not an outsider in our business. He is part of it. We are not doing him a favour by serving him. He is doing us a favour by giving us an opportunity to do so."*

NOTES/ACTION POINTS

_____

_____

_____

_____

_____

_____

_____

_____

_____

_____

_____

_____

_____

_____

NOTES/ACTION POINTS

_____

_____

_____

_____

_____

_____

_____

_____

_____

_____

_____

_____

_____

_____

_____

NOTES/ACTION POINTS

NOTES/ACTION POINTS

_____

_____

_____

_____

_____

_____

_____

_____

_____

_____

_____

_____

_____

_____

INDEX

How to contact Laurie Mellor regarding Training/Speaking

To book Laurie Mellor for Sales Training, Mentoring, Convention speaking, etc., please contact him c/o the Publishers:

Dream Depot Ltd.
P.O. Box No. 3218
Littlehampton
West Sussex, BN16 1WH
Tel: +44 (0)1903 859993
Fax: +44 (0)1903 859066
E-mail: office@dreamdepot.co.uk